ELIOT'S
MIDDLEMARCH

Continuum *Reader's Guides*

Continuum's *Reader's Guides* are clear, concise and accessible introductions to classic works of philosophy. Each book explores the major themes, historical and philosophical context and key passages of a major philosophical text, guiding the reader toward a thorough understanding of often demanding material. Ideal for undergraduate students, the guides provide an essential resource for anyone who needs to get to grips with a philosophical text.

Achebe's *Things Fall Apart* – Ode Ogede
Chaucer's *The Canterbury Tales* – Gail Ashton
Conrad's *Heart of Darkness* – Allan Simmons
Dickens's *Great Expectations* – Ian Brinton
Fitzgerald's *The Great Gatsby* – Nicolas Tredell
Fowles's *The French Lieutenant's Woman* – William Stephenson
Salinger's *The Catcher in the Rye* – Sarah Graham
William Blake's *Poetry* – Jonathan Roberts

ELIOT'S *MIDDLEMARCH*

Reader's Guide

JOSIE BILLINGTON

continuum

Continuum
The Tower Building   80 Maiden Lane
11 York Road   Suite 704
London SE1 7NX   New York, NY 10038
www.continuumbooks.com

British Library Cataloguing-in-Publication Data
A catalogue record for this book is available from the British Library.

ISBN: 978-0-8264-9551-8 (hardback)
      978-0-8264-9552-5 (paperback)

Typeset by Servis Filmsetting Ltd, Manchester
Printed and bound in Great Britain by
MPG Books Ltd, Bodmin, Cornwall

TABLE OF CONTENTS

ACKNOWLEDGEMENTS

I would like to thank Professor Chris Walsh, Professor Glyn Turton and colleagues from the University of Chester for permission to reproduce material that originally appeared in *George Eliot's Middlemarch: A Guide for Students and Readers of the Novel*. Thanks are also due to Jane Davis, Philip Davis, Alison Platt, Alan Shelston, Jackie Turton and Michael Davis for their wisdom, help or support at various stages of this project. I would also like to thank Anna Sandeman and Colleen Coalter at Continuum for their supportive advice and patience.

NOTE ON EDITION

Page references are from the Oxford World's Classics edition of *Middlemarch*, edited by David Carroll, with an introduction by Felicia Bonaparte (Oxford: Oxford University Press, 1997).

CHAPTER 1

CONTEXTS

GEORGE ELIOT'S LIFE AND WORK

My books are deeply serious things to me, and come out of all the painful discipline, all the most hardly-learnt lessons of my past life. (*Letters*, iii, 187)

George Eliot was born Mary Ann Evans on 22 November 1819, the third and last child of Christiana and Robert Evans, land-agent and manager of the Arbury Estate in Warwickshire where Mary Ann grew up. The author's childhood certainly influenced the pastoral scenes of *Middlemarch*, where Caleb Garth is loosely based on Mary Ann's father, and where the English county tenantry and yeomanry that formed the adult community of her childhood provides the representative model for the traditional and narrowly provincial mindset of the populace of Middlemarch. Yet *Middlemarch* the novel is the crowning achievement of the adult who had decisively broken from the social and religious conservatism of her past. As a young woman, she lost her religious faith, and her initial principled refusal to accompany her father to church caused a major rift with the man she had always revered and loved. A decade or so later, she took the courageous decision to live openly with George Henry Lewes, a man who was already married and, for legal reasons, unable to obtain a divorce. This step consigned her to ostracism from respectable society and, most painfully for 'Marian Lewes', led to the complete loss of communication with her family.

Even from the first, the novelist-to-be of ordinary life had been too extraordinarily rich in spirit and gifts to fit easily or comfortably into tidy provincial categories of gender and class. From an early age she had shown a prodigious talent and appetite for learning, providing almost for herself the kind of education (including mastery of Greek and Latin as well as extensive study of European languages and literature) conventionally enjoyed by a privileged, university-educated male elite. Her decision, as an unprovided-for single woman following her father's death, to move from the provinces to London to try to make her living as a writer was as brave and risky as any she took.

Yet George Eliot was to call these early years 'the primal passionate store' of all her 'after good'.[1] They were distinguished by Mary Ann's particularly close relationship with her older brother Isaac and it has been speculated that the intensity of this relationship, and the author's 'pre-eminently exclusive disposition' with regard to her affections, was itself partly compensatory, substituting for the primary tenderness of an emotionally aloof mother. She showed 'from the earliest years, the trait that was most marked in her all through life, namely, the absolute need of some one person who should be all in all to her, and to whom she should be all in all' (Cross, i, 11), and the possibility of her emotional arrestedness in that childhood has been persuasively offered as an explanation for her late development as a novelist (Redinger, 27–65).

The emotional and intellectual frustrations of her young life – 'the absolute despair I suffered from of ever being able to achieve anything' (*Letters*, II, 155–6) – seem to have inhibited her imaginative talents and expression in ways which were profoundly to shape her style: 'She complained of being troubled by double consciousness – a current of self-criticism being an habitual accompaniment of anything she was saying or doing; and this naturally tended towards self-depreciation and distrust. Probably it was this last trait which prevented her from displaying her powers and knowledge.'[2] Perhaps 'her release from creative inhibition' (Hardy [2006] 100) came not so much in freedom from that critical consciousness as in its transmutation into the presiding consciousness of her novels: 'The chief centre of interest for the imagination', said an early reviewer of her work, 'is that "second self" who writes her books, and lives and speaks through them'.[3] Possibly the clearest summary of how Mary Ann Evans suffering introspection became the humane rational voice we call 'George Eliot' comes from a contemporary novel in the writer's own realist tradition: 'George Eliot . . . was a good hater,' says Stephanie in A. S. Byatt's *Still Life*. 'She looked long and intelligently at what she hated, with curiosity to see exactly *what* it was, and the necessary detachment to imagine it from within and without, these two breeding a kind of knowledge that was love.'[4]

The writing career of Marian Evans[5] was as an essayist, translator and literary journalist. Within a short time of settling in London, she had become effective editor of the *Westminster Review*, restoring the journal's damaged reputation by raising its intellectual level to a new pre-eminence. Her first fiction, *Scenes of Clerical Life*, was published in 1856, several years after her union with Lewes. It was no accident that the emergence of 'George Eliot' came so soon after her transformation into 'Marian Lewes'. Her correspondence of the 1850s indicates that with Lewes, at the age of 36, Marian had found the intellectual and emotional fulfilment that she had craved for most of her life. From the outset, they developed a mutually supportive, even collaborative mode of pursuing their nonetheless independent intellectual pursuits, which set the pattern for the remainder of their lives together. There is no question that it was Lewes who first encouraged her to try her hand at fiction, and little doubt that it was the confidence inspired by his support and his belief in her powers that persuaded her to take this further momentous step in her life. It is also the case that his greater practical experience of (and ease in) dealing with the literary and publishing worlds smoothed her path considerably.

The work that was to have formed a further 'Scene' of Clerical Life became George Eliot's first novel *Adam Bede*, published in 1859. It was an instant success, both critically and financially, and established George Eliot as one of the leading novelists of the day. Fame and literary respect did not bring social acceptance, all the more because it made it impossible for her to preserve her incognito. The adoption of a male pseudonym – itself an apparent tribute to (George) Lewes – was motivated by the author's fear of criticism and considerations of gender, but also by the fact that her relationship with Lewes, widely-known and condemned, would compromise, and perhaps even prevent altogether, a fair hearing for her work. Yet her success as a novelist grew, with the publication of *The Mill on the Floss* (1860), *Silas Marner* (1861), *Romola* (1862) and *Felix Holt, the Radical* (1865). *Middlemarch*, published in 1871–2, was a commercial and critical triumph, and the acme of George Eliot's writing career. The acclaim consolidated George Eliot's reputation as the greatest living novelist, and from this time she was accepted fully into society, drawing the admiration of Queen Victoria. George Eliot published her last novel *Daniel Deronda* in 1876 and her final work, *The Impressions of Theophrastus Such*, in 1879.

When Lewes died of a sudden attack of illness in 1879, a devastated Marian went into self-imposed seclusion for months, communicating with no one but John Cross (the Lewes's close friend and regular visitor, upon whose support she became increasingly dependent during this time), and undertaking to complete Lewes's unpublished manuscript *Problems of Life and Mind*. When she emerged from the labour of this tribute and from her grief-stricken solitude, she married John Cross, 20 years her junior, in May 1880 and for the second time shocked her friends by the conduct of her personal life. The union, however, brought the long-awaited reconciliation with her brother Isaac, who wrote congratulating her on her marriage. Later that same year, on 22 December, Marian died after a brief illness. Refused burial in Westminster Abbey, she was buried next to Lewes in Highgate Cemetery.

INTELLECTUAL AND CULTURAL CONTEXTS

Secularization

One paradox of the Victorian period is that it was simultaneously an age of faith and an age of increasingly widespread doubt and lost belief. On the one hand, more chapels and churches were built than at any time before or since; the religious press flourished; millions of copies of tracts and sermons were published by religious societies; it was the great age of the communal hymn and theological questions and ecclesiastical controversies were the subject of intense debate. On the other hand, agnosticism or religious doubt replaced religious faith as the keynote of the age: industrial and technological advances encouraged materialist values and ambitions to supplant spiritual ones; developments in philosophy, the sciences and biblical studies threatened to undermine the very foundations of the Christian religion and there was a general feeling that the century's soul had lost its way. As the poet Matthew Arnold put it in 'The Study of Poetry' (1880): 'There is not a creed which is not shaken, not an accredited dogma which is not shown to be questionable, not a received tradition which does not threaten to dissolve.'[6]

To understand much of the broad cultural background to

Middlemarch one need look no further than its author's own religious and intellectual development. In this respect, as Basil Willey has famously said, George Eliot's biography offers 'a paradigm . . . a graph, of [the century's] most decided trend' (Haight, 260): the profoundly shaking experience of turning from committed belief, to doubt, or loss of Christian faith, that was undergone by a whole generation of educated middle-class Victorian thinkers. As an adolescent Mary Ann was swept up in the religious current of Evangelicalism – a passionate, earnest, totalizing belief which in the first half of the nineteenth century had a profound impact not just on the rural towns of England but on English cultural and intellectual life in general. It was when she moved from the Arbury Estate to Coventry at the age of 22 that Mary Ann was introduced to an intellectual circle that had an immediate, profound and decisive influence on the future direction of her thought and life, placing it on a new philosophical axis. The Brays and Hennels were wealthy tradespeople, whose dissenting Unitarian liberal tradition put them in the vanguard of middle-class progressive thought. Mary Ann quickly came into contact with the chief intellectual currents and controversies of her age, and most especially the challenges presented to traditional religious faith by evolutionary science and by German historical scholarship on Christianity, which radically disputed the Bible's claims to be an authentic historical record. (This 'higher criticism' is the same scholarship which, as Will Ladislaw explains to Dorothea Brook in *Middlemarch*, makes Mr Casaubon's search for 'the key to all mythologies' a futile endeavour.) Moreover, she was surrounded by thinkers who were seeking to come to a rationalistic understanding of the whole phenomenon of Christianity, or were conscientiously seeking to forge systems of thought that could humanely replace those which rested upon a belief in God. Charles Hennel's book *An Enquiry Concerning the Origin of Christianity* (1838) repudiated the biblical accounts of miracles and explained the life of Jesus solely in historical terms, avowing that the life showed no deviation from the known laws of nature. Charles Bray's guiding ideas were worked out in his book *The Philosophy of Necessity; or, the Law of Consequences as applicable to Mental, Moral and Social Science* (1840), where he expounded his determinist philosophy that man's social, moral and mental life are subject to fixed and unalterable laws of cause and effect in just the same way as the phenomena of the physical world. In this substitution of a scientific explanation of human life for a religious one, the Brays and Hennels were part of the advance guard of a shift which was taking place throughout English society.

The most thorough critical account of the Bible was David Friedrich Strauss's *Das Leben Jesu*, the translation of which Mary Ann completed in 1846. It was the (anonymous) publication of this work that established her credentials as a writer and thinker, but letters from the period demonstrate that she struggled intensely not only with the linguistic challenge but with the project of committing to rationalist explanation such events as the crucifixion. While her intellectual sympathies increasingly endorsed the endeavour to understand the Bible not as the divinely inspired word of God but as 'a series of historical documents',[7] she felt an emotional antipathy to the rationalization of the human power and truth which the gospels still held for her. She found the key to translating Christian values into engaged secular humanism with her translation of Ludwig von Feuerbach's *The Essence of Christianity* (1854). Feuerbach argued that the virtuous qualities of love, charity, mercy and pity, which humans had projected onto God, were qualities and needs that belonged to humans themselves. Religion, he said, arose as the result of an urgent, imaginative need in humankind to objectify, in the form of a perfect, transcendental being, the very best qualities, the highest yearnings and feelings of humanity itself. As George Eliot put it in a letter of 1874: 'The idea of God so far as it has been a high spiritual influence, is the ideal of a goodness entirely human (i.e. an exaltation of the human)' (*Letters*, VI, 98). What was needful now, as Feuerbach saw it, was for humans to recognize that the qualities and strengths they had found in God were really their own. In that way, the human content of Christianity could be retained even while its form was rejected. 'With the ideas of Feuerbach,' Marian Evans wrote, 'I everywhere agree' (*Letters*, II, 153). In Feuerbach's work she had found a philosophical basis for preserving, in the form of humanist morality, what she valued in Christian theology, and the Feuerbachian influence is strong, as we shall see in the dynamics and very mechanics of *Middlemarch*.

Of perhaps equal, if less widely-acknowledged influence is the work of the enlightened rationalist philosopher Spinoza, whose *Ethics* Marian Evans translated in 1856 (though the translation was never published in her lifetime). Spinoza's conception of God as immanent in the universe, in all thoughts and objects, as opposed to the Judaeo-Christian concept of a supernatural creator, made aspects of his work forerunners of Feuerbach's 'religion of human-ity', and must have appealed to Marian Evans on those grounds alone. Yet *Ethics* is also a fascinating study of how thoughts trigger emotions and of how emotions become the kind of thoughts we call feelings. Reason was humanity's hope for Spinoza, because the only way of overcoming an irrational passion or negative emotion was by countering it with an even stronger positive emotion, brought about by reasoning and intellectual effort: 'Central to his thinking was the notion that the subduing of the passions should be accomplished by reason-induced emotion and not by pure reason alone.'[8] As we shall see, much of the moral vision of *Middlemarch*, including Dorothea's conquering of passion in Chapter 80, rests upon the Spinozan ethical system.

George Eliot began her career as a fiction writer at a time when the very form of human narrative was undergoing transformation, in ways as alienating and disconcerting as they were potentially liberating. George Eliot's first novel, *Adam Bede*, was published in the same year as Charles Darwin's *The Origin of Species*, the definitive expression of evolutionary theory. Suddenly human history did not begin 'In the beginning' at the Creation in Genesis, with a divinely ordered shape and teleology; instead the human species was the arbitrary outcome of the transmutation of species, and its purpose was as a procreative agent of evolutionary process:

> Time was longer – almost infinitely longer – than had been imag-ined. Human beings and their communities were slow growths, comparable to shells and forests. The idea of progress carried with it the idea of redundancy and extinction ... [In *Middlemarch*, George Eliot] is writing what ... she called the 'Natural History' of the life of communities. A natural history is very different from the Saint's life which Dorothea Brooke wanted so ardently to inhabit.[9]

In thus paying homage simultaneously to a human and evolutionary perspective, as well as observing the tensions between them, George Eliot was drawing upon the 'passionate store' of her own adoles-cent, frustrated, passionate needs and the sophisticated scientific philosophy which was the milieu of her adult life. One of the most influential lifelong friendships Marian formed while editing the *Westminster Review* was with Herbert Spencer, considered by many of his contemporaries to be the foremost thinker and philosopher of his time. Greatly influenced by Darwin, Spencer became the founder of evolutionary philosophy, seeking to explicate all aspects of existence according to evolutionary theory. Positing a gradual movement from the homogeneous to the heterogeneous, the simple to the complex, Spencer viewed history as fundamentally progressive, and characterized in its natural forms by the gradual adjustment of the inner organizations of organisms to external conditions. *Middlemarch*, as we shall see, is scrupulously minute in its examination of the process of adjustment of inward drive and disposition to delimiting, distorting or chastening social forms or structures. Yet a great deal of the complex energy of *Middlemarch*, at once signalled and harnessed by its rich and abundant weblike imagery, derives from its responsiveness to an evolutionary model of life as intricately arbitrary and various, unplanned and unpredictable, and susceptible to infinite overlap, collision and connection.

The Rise of the Novel

The Victorian period was the age of the novel as distinctly as the Romantic period that preceded it had been the age of poetry. The dominance of the novel form is clear from the vast numbers which were produced: tens of thousands of separate titles were published between 1837 and 1901, such that Anthony Trollope, himself a prolific novelist, could say in 1870: 'We have become a novel-reading people. Novels are in the hands of us all; from the Prime Minister down to the last-appointed scullery maid.'[10] But it was more than the quantity and massive popularity of novels that was new. The quality of these works, the huge literary achievement they represented, was equally unprecedented. A form which had had individual successes in the early nineteenth century in the work of Jane Austen and Walter Scott, now had a new and major generation, whose names – Dickens, Gaskell, the Brontës, George Eliot, Thomas Hardy – continue to be synonymous with the idea of the great English novel.

Socio-economic conditions enabled production of large numbers of novels in the period. New methods of binding and printing brought book process costs down; there were cheap new libraries; the reading of newspapers and magazines was increasing rapidly.

Serial publication of fiction in the monthly part and in the new family magazines was significantly expanding the number of readers of novels. Moreover, the Industrial Revolution had strengthened the position of the middle class who, given the general level of literacy in England before the 1870 Education Act (which universalized education), made up the majority of the novel-reading public. Recently enfranchised by the Reform Bill of 1832, this newly expanded and increasingly powerful and prosperous commercial class were impatient with the kind of heroes and heroines who upheld the values of the older, privileged aristocracy which the middle classes were in the process of superseding. They wanted to read books that related to their own lives and were peopled by ordinary individuals whose virtues and interests were not those of princely courage or military heroism, but of unextraordinary professional and domestic life. In keeping with the politics of the age, the novel was a democratic form, treating the individual soul of whatever rank as inherently significant.

The secular, inclusive form of the novel – 'the epic of a world that has been abandoned by God'[11] – was precisely suited to George Eliot's expansiveness of vision. The *novel* was exactly that in the nineteenth century – a *new* form, which had no settled form, and which could exploit its freedom from canonical laws and classical definitions, and the flexible informality of prose discourse itself, to become whatever it wanted to be. In an age of unprecedented social change, in which rapid urbanization, industrialization and technological innovation were the pre-conditions of the Victorian period's related upheavals in politics and religion, a whole generation of readers and writers seized on a form of literature that was large and loose enough to contain the amplitude of their contemporary experience. By the 1870s, when *Middlemarch* was published, Britain had enjoyed two decades of rising prosperity and commercial and manufacturing dominance. As if in cultural testimony to that material confidence, this period witnessed the supreme achievements in the Victorian realist form. By widening its own scope as a genre, the novel had annexed to itself the interpretation of human experience in the context of time, space and circumstance which had hitherto been the function of philosophy, history, poetry and natural science. *Middlemarch* is a work that helped to seal the cultural authority of the novel in the modern world.

SOCIAL AND POLITICAL CONTEXTS

Reform

Together with the massive increase in population during the Victorian age (by 1851 the population of England and Wales had doubled in comparison to the start of the century, and was virtually to double again by 1901) and the spectacular growth of the industrial city, the establishment of a national railway network helped accelerate migration from rural to urban centres, in the process literally changing the face of the English landscape, as well as customary notions of time and distance. While industrial centres and the railway engine were symbols of the awesome power of technology and the material progress of the nation, the rate and extent of change caused social upheaval on a profound and colossal scale as older communities, traditions and values were fragmented and haphazardly reconstituted. Political instability was also a threat, as the middle classes increasingly articulated their demand that their economic contribution to the country's developing economy be rewarded by influence in government. The working classes too were agitating for a political voice, and the prospect of an English equivalent of the French Revolution disturbed the middle-class supporters of the liberal-democratic Whig party as much as it appalled the ruling, aristocratic Tory administration.

The political reforms of the 1830s were designed principally to preserve political stability and improve administrative efficiency in the face of widespread social and economic change. Nonetheless they constitute a watershed in British history, marking the end of the feudal, decentralized form of government that disabled collective and coherent public policy, and the beginning of a more responsive, parliamentary attitude to the public will. The return of a Whig administration in the election of 1831 began a period of increasing government intervention in areas such as education, health, social order and employment, which lasted to the end of the century. The key piece of legislation that initiated this spirit of public reform was the Great Reform Act of 1832, which extended representation to the middle classes. Further extension of voting rights, however, was not granted until the second reform act of 1867.

George Eliot was thus writing *Middlemarch* in the aftermath of one period of parliamentary change, the passing of the 1867 Reform Act, and looking back to pre-Victorian times, to the confused and not dissimilar events preceding the Great Reform Act of 1832. In the early chapters of *Middlemarch* the author goes to careful lengths to place the events depicted within the novel at this particular point in English history: 'Most of the historical references in the novel concern events and personalities involved in the struggle for political reform which culminated in the passage of the First Reform Bill in June 1832.'[12] The novel begins in the autumn of 1829, covers the collapse of the Tory administration and the installation of a Whig government in 1830, the general election of 1831, and ends in the early summer of 1832, after the Lords had thrown out the Reform Bill, and less than two months before the Act was finally passed. It is this climax in the national life, and the period leading up to the adoption of the Bill, which *Middlemarch* partly chronicles. George Eliot's notebook for the novel and her journal entries show that in addition to her careful research of the stages in the passage of the Reform Bill, she extensively researched the medical horizons and controversies, as well as the specific medical practices and discoveries of the 1820s and 1830s. Thus, 'the medical strand was clearly an integral part of the novel's underlying theme of reform and transition'.[13]

Reform was the nineteenth century's 'social faith' (*Middlemarch*, 3), in place of a religious one. Lydgate, the zealous medical reformer, and to a lesser extent Ladislaw, the Radical politician, are types of the pioneers living in the 1830s whose struggles helped to bring about the world of the 1870s. Ladislaw's and Lydgate's status as outsiders in Middlemarch ('There is no stifling,' says Lydgate, 'the offence of being young, and a new-comer, and happening to know something more than the old inhabitants', 434) connects them to the larger forces of the outside world, which are shown to be making their impact on the old provincial world: 'In the hundred to which Middlemarch belonged railways were as exciting a topic as the Reform Bill or the imminent horrors of Cholera' (544). The hayforks with which the labourers make their offensive approach to the railway agents are a sort of literal analogue of the town's opposition to Lydgate's practices and the medical profession's intransigent refusal to collaborate on the new hospital, as well as the gentry's antagonism to reformist politics.

What seems to have attracted George Eliot to the years 1829 to 1832 is that this was a period in which so many areas of national life – political, scientific, economic, philanthropic – were undergoing, or were on the eve of, reform. Moreover, these were the years that ushered in the subsequent period of far-reaching and often tumultuous social, economic and political change, through which the author and many of her readers had lived. It is as if George Eliot were turning back to the originating moments in history that had shaped the contemporary world of her own day: 'George Eliot is seeking a starting-point, the origins of the strong currents that had modified her social, political, and cultural environment.'[14] There were specific reasons for doing so in the late 1860s and early 1870s: 1867 had seen the passing of the Second Reform Bill (which further extended the franchise, and caused alarm among certain sectors of Victorian society). The time of the novel's composition, therefore, is not only the historical product of, but also analogous to, the period which the novel covers, and this parallel has a material effect on the novel's sense of closure. At one level, the Finale of the novel places the characters and their world in a historically superseded past, even as it depicts them marching positively into the future. (The marriage of Will Ladislaw and Dorothea Brooke takes place at the same time as the passing of the First Reform Bill. Thus Dorothea's rejection – in sacrificing Casaubon's wealth – of a conservative past and Tory principles of landed privilege, and her embrace – in marrying Will – of the principle of reform and the liberal values of the future, are paralleled in the historical life of the nation as a whole.) Yet the 'double time' that George Eliot creates within the novel – 'the "now" of herself and her first readers and the "now-then" of the late 1820s' (Beer, 1986, 152) – encourages her contemporary readers to see the ambitions of their own age in relation to the failures or muted successes recorded in the Finale. Precisely at the point where the novel seems to be suggesting that these lives are a closed book, and irrevocably past, the novel is therefore also bringing them into resonant connection with the present, by implicitly suggesting the continuance of their concerns into the late nineteenth century. What looks like closure proves to be its opposite, denying finality in a post-heroic age for such problems in respect of reform that Dorothea, Lydgate, Ladislaw and others variously represent.

The Woman Question

The Victorian period initiated unprecedented public debate about the role and position of women. The place of woman in family and society had been more or less secured and taken for granted in a pre-Victorian world where God was the final reference point. Many traditional ideologies persisted into and throughout the Victorian age, particularly the view that a woman's natural vocation was as wife, mother and helpmate, and that men and women's aptitudes and roles were biologically distinct. In the great explosive, melting pot of Victorian society, however, the guy ropes were up and the function, role and identity of woman was being renegotiated in almost every area of public life – legislation, educational and employment opportunity, and in the field of literature, where for the first time women writers came into their own. Thus in the early 1850s, when George Eliot was herself a young woman seeking emancipation through ideas, a women's suffrage petition was presented to the house of Lords, a significant legal judgement ruled that a man may not force his wife to live with him, and George Henry Lewes published an article entitled 'The Lady Novelists', which drew attention to the flourishing phenomenon of the professional female writer. The year before George Eliot began writing *Middlemarch* saw the founding of the first woman's college, Girton in Cambridge, the first Married Woman's Property Act (which overturned the doctrine of spousal unity whereby a wife had no legal identity or property rights apart from her husband), an Education Act securing the right of women to serve on school boards, and the publication of John Stuart Mill's hugely influential *The Subjection of Women*. Mill's thesis turned on its head the question of whether women were the weaker sex by arguing that if women were indeed less capable than men, laws excluding them from career and professional life were unnecessary, since their incompetence would find them out in the competitive market place.

One further effect of having set her novel back in time is that the female characters George Eliot depicts are even more restricted socially and economically than the women of her own age, so the frustration of vocational ambition which, in the Prelude to the novel, is described as 'the social lot of woman', is brought into sharper focus. The middle-class liberal-intellectual circles in which Marian Evans moved as a young woman in Coventry and later in London brought her into close and sustained contact both with issues relating to the 'Woman Question' and with the increasing number of articles, studies and pamphlets which debated it, and with many of the women who were most actively involved in drawing attention to it. Not only did she meet with some of the most influential campaigners for female rights (Florence Nightingale among them), almost every woman to whom she was close from the 1850s onwards was taking an active part in the woman's movement, with some of them leading it. Two of her closest friends were Bessie Parkes and Barbara Leigh-Smith, whose energetic campaigns on behalf of the legal, political and educational rights of women were both admired and, to an extent, practically supported by George Eliot. She subscribed from the outset to *The English Women's Review*, the journal founded in 1857 by Barbara Leigh-Smith, and edited by Bessie Parkes, believing that 'it must be doing good substantially – stimulating women to useful work, and rousing people generally to some consideration of women's needs'. She signed Barbara Leigh-Smith's petition to Parliament relating to married women's property rights, seeing it as an important step in a lengthy and gradual process of reform 'stretching far beyond our lives'. She donated £50 towards the establishment of Girton in 1869, avowing that 'the better Education of Women is one of the objects about which I have *no doubt*'. Later she wrote in justification of her contribution to the foundation of the college: 'Women ought to have the same store of truth placed within their reach as men have . . . the same store of fundamental knowledge' (*Letters*, iii, 225; ii, 227; iv, 339; v, 58). Her essay 'Woman in France' (1854) concludes with a similar injunction that 'the whole field of reality be laid open to woman as well as to man', and her review (1855) of Margaret Fuller (nineteenth-century feminist author and critic) and Mary Wollstonecraft (eighteenth-century radical and feminist) stresses the profound importance, for men and women alike, of 'the removal of unjust laws and artificial restrictions, so that the possibilities of [woman's] nature may have room for full development' (Ashton, 1992, 68; 180).

There is no question that George Eliot shared the feminist movement's intolerance of the exclusion of women from knowledge and educational opportunities, as well as its resentment at the inequalities between men and women that were inscribed in legal and political institutions. Yet George Eliot's support for reform was as cautious as it was ambivalent. In 1857, she wrote: 'I should be sorry to undertake any specific enunciation of doctrine on a question so entangled as the "Woman Question".' And at the height of her fame she still refused to take a radical or ideologically partisan stance on the issue of women's rights, partly on the grounds of its complexity, and partly out of a belief that pronouncements on the woman question did 'not come well from' her: 'There are many points of this kind that want being urged, but . . . I never like to be quoted in any way on this subject' (*Letters*, ii, 396; iv, 425). Her reluctance publicly and unequivocally to state her position, or to give active and open support to the campaign for female rights, was apparently in part the result of her compromised social position as the partner of George Henry Lewes and a fear, perhaps, that support from a woman who had lost social respect and reputation would endanger rather than promote the female cause.

Yet George Eliot's agnosticism on the 'woman question' and her aloofness from the woman's movement seems more squarely to find its basis in her sense of the specificity of female talents. In 'Woman in France' she attempted to define the special qualities she believed women of all ages and cultures to possess by virtue of their 'distinctively feminine condition': 'Under every imaginable social condition, she will necessarily have a class of sensations and emotions – the maternal ones – which must remain unknown to man' (Ashton, 37). In her otherwise scathing essay 'Silly Novels by Lady Novelists' (1856), the author concludes her essay affirmatively by acknowledging that 'women can produce novels not only fine, but among the very finest', and these 'finest' novels 'have a precious speciality, lying quite apart from masculine aptitudes and experience' (ibid. 320). Her resistance to female suffrage and to thorough-going equality for men and women stems from a belief in sexual difference founded on biology, maternity and domesticity, whose contribution was not confined to the domestic sphere, but which extended in its social and moral benefits across an entire culture:

> As a mere zoological evolution, woman seems to me to have the worst share in existence. But for that very reason I would the more contend that in the moral evolution of women we have 'an art which does mend nature' – an art which 'itself is nature'. It is the function of love in the largest sense to mitigate the harshness of all fatalities. (*Letters*, iv, 402–3)

At its most effective, greater learning and opportunity for women would allow the full development of women's potential while safeguarding, and even enhancing, her special qualities. In her review of Wollstonecraft, she quotes the latter affirmatively thus:

' "I contend that the heart would expand as the understanding gained, if women were not depressed from their cradles" ' (Ashton, 1992, 186).

Yet change, to be effective, enduring and rewarding to society as a whole, would need to be slow and piecemeal, and in this respect George Eliot's pronouncements on the woman question read like a blueprint for the vision of reform offered in *Middlemarch*:

> On the one side we hear that woman's position can never be improved until women themselves are better; and, on the other, that women can never become better until their position is improved . . . But we constantly hear the same difficulty stated about the human race in general. There is a perpetual action and reaction between individuals and institutions; we must try to mend little by little – the only way in which human things can be mended. (Ibid.)

George Eliot's emphasis on wide, and human rather than gender-specific amelioration is present in the dual narrative of Dorothea and Lydgate: 'It might be pointed out to those who . . . see in *Middlemarch* chiefly the drama of a woman's failure that the novel is concerned almost equally [in Lydgate] with the thwarting of a man's efforts' (Ashton, 1983, 71). The novel's inclusive emphasis is equally present, as we shall see more fully in Chapter 2, in the non-sectarianism of the narrative voice: '[George Eliot's] persistent use of "we" is not liberal but stringent, binding us across categories and collapsing privileged distance. The "we" of her text moves, often with deliberate disturbance, askance gender, class, and time' (Beer, 1986, 28–9).

NOTES

1 From 'Brother and Sister Sonnets', 5, (1874): see Byatt (1990), 429.
2 Herbert Spencer, *Autobiography*. London: Williams and Norgate, 386–7.
3 Edward Dowden (1872) in Haight (1965), 64; Carroll (1971), 321.
4 A. S. Byatt (1985), *Still Life*. London: Chatto and Windus, 52.
5 As she was now signing her name. See Rosemarie Bodenheimer, 'A Woman of Many Names' in Levine (2001), 26.
6 Matthew Arnold, 'The Study of Poetry' (1880) in *Essays in Criticism*, Second Series (London: Macmillan, 1888), p. 1.

7 'Evangelical Teaching: Dr Cumming' (1855) in Ashton (1992), 150.
8 Antonio Demasio (2003), *Looking for Spinoza*. London: William Heinemann, 12.
9 A. S. Byatt (1999) 'Introduction' to *Middlemarch*. Oxford World's Classics. Oxford: Oxford University Press, vi.
10 Anthony Trollope, 'On English Prose as a Rational Amusement, in Morris L. Parish (ed.), *Four Lectures* (London: Constable, 1938).
11 Anna Bostock trans. (1971) and Georg Lukács (1920) *The Theory of the Novel*. London: Merlin Press, 41.
12 Jerome Beaty, 'History by Indirection: The Era of Reform' in Haight, 306.
13 Lilian R. Furst (1993) 'Struggling for Medical Reform in *Middlemarch*' in *Nineteenth-Century Literature*, 48, iii, 242.
14 Michael Mason (1971), '*Middlemarch* and History', *Nineteenth-Century Fiction*, vol. 25, 418.

STUDY QUESTIONS

1 In Chapter 15 of the novel, George Eliot describes herself as a 'belated historian' who must concentrate on 'this particular web' of 'human lots'. In her notebooks, George Eliot transcribed the following passage from the Victorian historian Macauley: 'He alone reads history aright, who . . . learns to distinguish what is accidental and transitory in human nature, from what is essential and immutable.' Does George Eliot in *Middlemarch* 'fulfil as a novelist Macauley's prescription for the historian' (see Wheeler, 137)?

2. '*Middlemarch* is the product of George Eliot's effort to sustain existence at two levels, bringing together what it feels like at ground level (in character) and what it feels like from above (in the creator). But in *Middlemarch* there is an author always drawn back down inside her characters, and there are characters who are frequently struggling on the verge of some semi-transcendent or external view of themselves' (Davis, 387). Consider George Eliot's use of ideas in the light of this account of the novel's creative-intellectual dynamic.

CHAPTER 2

LANGUAGE, STYLE, GENRE

In Chapter 20 of *Middlemarch*, Dorothea, unhappily honeymooning in Italy with her husband, is traumatized and alienated by her presence among the ruins of Rome, which offer, unconsciously enough, an image of the dreadful disappointment her marriage is proving to be:

> Not that this inward amazement of Dorothea's was anything very exceptional: many souls in their young nudity are tumbled out among incongruities and left to 'find their feet' among them, while their elders go about their business. Nor can I suppose that when Mrs Casaubon is discovered in a fit of weeping six weeks after her wedding, the situation will be regarded as tragic. Some discouragement, some faintness of heart at the new real future which replaces the imaginary, is not unusual, and we do not expect people to be deeply moved by what is not unusual. That element of tragedy which lies in the very fact of frequency, has not yet wrought itself into the coarse emotion of mankind; and perhaps our frames could hardly bear much of it. If we had a keen vision and feeling of all ordinary human life, it would be like hearing the grass grow and the squirrel's heart beat, and we should die of that roar which lies on the other side of silence. As it is, the quickest of us walk about well wadded with stupidity. (191–2)

No novel in English before *Middlemarch* had been so dedicated to *not* passing over in silence the hidden 'roar' of ordinary human suffering. George Eliot's 'penetration into the recesses of the commonplace and of the else undiscovered deeps'[1] in *Middlemarch* sealed her reputation as a great psychological novelist and, as was recognized by her contemporaries, introduced a new departure and development for the novel as a genre.[2] Yet the novel here powerfully acknowledges the necessary inability of an ordinary human in ordinary life to be anything other than desensitized to the inner tragedy of Dorothea's situation: 'Our frames could hardly bear much of it . . . we should die.' *Middlemarch* is the outcome of George Eliot's own inability, for all her intellectual acceptance of the evolutionary necessity of such 'stupidity', to 'bear' to leave her readership thus underevolved.

A *tour de force* of psychological realism, *Middlemarch* is also a moral project or 'experiment' (*Letters*, vi, 216), dedicated to using its penetrative exactitude of psychological insight to try to uncoarsen the sensibilities of its readers. What has been called George Eliot's 'aesthetic of sympathy' was announced in an essay, 'The Natural History of German Life' (1856), which has come to be accepted as a manifesto of the novelist's own position as a writer:

> The greatest benefit we owe to the artist, whether painter, poet or novelist, is the extension of our sympathies . . . Appeals founded on generalisations and statistics require a sympathy ready-made, a moral sentiment already in activity; but a picture of human life such as a great artist can give, surprises even the trivial and the selfish into that attention to what is apart from themselves, which may be called the raw material of moral sentiment. (Ashton, 1992, 263)

In the year her first novel was published she wrote:

> If Art does not enlarge men's sympathies, it does nothing morally . . . the only effect I ardently long to produce by my writings, is that those who read them should be able to *imagine* and to *feel* the pains and the joys of those who differ from themselves in everything but the broad fact of being struggling erring human creatures. (*Letters*, iii, 111)

George Eliot's moral project permeates every level of *Middlemarch*: its dynamics of language and structure cannot be explained in the absence of her moral aesthetic, for it is the anchor of the book, just as moral humanism was the anchor of her life when she lost belief in God.

Indeed, the project is visible even where, as in the passage under discussion here, it appears to announce its own defeat. The opening two sentences of this paragraph invoke a common sense view of Dorothea's situation – as nothing 'very exceptional' – without entirely endorsing that view or inviting the reader to do so. Just sufficient distance is created by, for instance, the quotation marks around that cliché ' "find their feet" ' to give this elders' perspective the air of unconsidered banality and to forestall our identification with the narrator's apparent acquiescence in it ('Not that this inward amazement' . . . 'Nor can I suppose'). When that 'I' becomes 'we' in the third sentence – 'we do not expect people to be deeply moved by what is not unusual' – the ironic aloofness encouraged in the first two sentences aligns the reader with 'we' as against 'people', urging the reader to recognize his or her own possible limitation of understanding rather than be merely subject to it. The next sentence subsumes 'we' in the category 'mankind', thus widening a (non-ironic) surplus perspective, yet without sacrificing sympathetic identification with the incapacity of 'our frames' vicariously to tolerate others' suffering.

This paragraph is not simply preaching, as George Eliot's narrative voice, we shall see, is often accused of doing. Rather, in situating the narrating and reading mind as if inside and outside those mortal limitations at once, its rhetorical strategies seek to open up a negotiable, meditative space on the borderline between writer and reader, novel and ordinary life. The prose evokes a sort of collaborative consciousness that operates like a third dimension, where the recognition of limitation can amount to something other than limitation merely – something more like sensitive moral expansion. As we shall see more fully in the second part of this chapter and in Chapter 2, the narration thus enjoins the reader to the kind of evolution that the narrative forces upon its characters. The first section of this chapter will demonstrate how George Eliot's desire to make room for that transactional, meditative-emotional space influenced the language of the novel.

VOICES AND MODES

Dorothea

The reader's introduction to Dorothea in the early chapters of the novel is a good example of how a surplus perspective is kept in play. Dorothea is first introduced via the conventional banalities which the paragraph above at first deploys: 'She was usually spoken of as being remarkably clever, but with the addition that her sister Celia had more common sense' (7). Quite quickly the narration begins to ventriloquize this reproving view:

A young lady of some birth and fortune, who knelt suddenly down on a brick floor by the side of a sick labourer and prayed fervidly as if she thought herself living in the time of the Apostles – who had strange whims of fasting like a Papist, and of sitting up at night to read old theological books! (9)

The reproachful sarcasm directed at Dorothea is itself ironized here, the more especially when in the next sentence it becomes clear that the narration is not impersonating the tone, view and language of Middlemarch society in general but of the male members of society who regard themselves as Dorothea's potential suitors:

Such a wife might awaken you one fine morning with a new scheme for the application of her income which would interfere with polit-ical economy and the keeping of saddle-horses: a man would natu-rally think twice before he risked himself in such fellowship. (ibid.)

So long as these critical reactions to Dorothea are the responsibility of someone other than the narrator, the reader is forced to reserve acquiescence in them. Reservation and unsettlement are now com-pounded as the narration semi-ironically ventriloquizes Dorothea's point of view, and seems to vindicate Middlemarch society's esti-mate of Dorothea's religious enthusiasms as self-dramatizing and self-delusive:

Most men thought her bewitching when she was on horseback. She loved the fresh air and the various aspects of the country, and when her eyes and cheeks glowed with mingled pleasures she looked very much like a devotee. Riding was an indulgence which she allowed herself in spite of conscientious qualms; she felt that she enjoyed it in a pagan sensuous way, and always looked forward to renouncing it. (10)

The narration apparently distances itself equally from the prejudices of Middlemarch society and from Dorothea's naive ardour. In fact, as with the putative suitor in the passage above, the closer the narration gets to Dorothea's own thoughts and language the more subtly powerful its implicit criticism of her religious fervour becomes. In the last sentence the voice and language of the narrator mixes almost inseparably with that of the character, ambiguously merging at 'she felt', and situating the remainder of the sentence at once inside Dorothea's subjectivism and outside it, as objectivizing witness.

This mode of narration, which hovers between first and third person as if poised between character and narrator (sometimes called *free indirect mode*), was not new to the English novel when George Eliot made use if it in *Middlemarch*: but its usage in this novel is so extensive and virtuoso as to have had an incalculable influence upon the future development of the novel in England (Pascal, 81). The incremental subtlety of its effect can be discerned in the paragraph immediately succeeding the extract quoted above:

> Dorothea, with all her eagerness to know the truths of life, retained very childlike ideas about marriage. She felt sure she would have accepted the judicious Hooker, if she had been born in time to save him from that wretched mistake he made in matrimony; or John Milton when his blindness had come on; or any of the other great men whose odd habits it would have been glorious piety to endure; but an amiable handsome baronet, who said 'Exactly' to her remarks even when she expressed uncertainty – how could he affect her as a lover? The really delightful marriage must be that where your husband was a sort of father, and could teach you even Hebrew, if you wished it. (10)

The shift to free indirect speech happens, once again, at that ambiguous 'she felt', before which the prose carries the stamp of the narrator's authority. From this point onwards, as David Lodge points out in his influential analysis of this passage, 'the narrator's discourse becomes permeated with Dorothea's discourse . . . without ever succumbing to it':

> The fact is that mimesis [the language of the character] and diegesis [the language of the narrator] are fused together inextricably here, and for good purpose. For there is a sense in which Dorothea knows what the narrator knows – namely, that

Sir James is sexually attracted to her – but is repressing the thought, on account of her determination to marry an intellectual father-figure.[3]

The same purpose that Lodge identifies here might be attributed to the use of free indirect mode in the previous paragraph, where Dorothea also 'knows', at one level, like the narrator, that her feeling that 'she enjoyed horse-riding in a pagan sensuous way' is a rather dubious justification for a pleasure which is inconsistent with her religious principles. Yet in both examples the view of the narrator and of the character also remain separate, to the degree that Dorothea, in her youthful zeal, *does* succumb – is naively convinced by – her own self-justifications, in a way that the narrator's mature ironic wisdom does not.

It is the paradoxical and simultaneous closeness and separateness of these voices which makes them together a powerful weapon of critical sympathy: 'The reader oscillate[s] between an emotional identification with characters and an obliquely judicious response to their situation.'[4] The oscillation is crucial to George Eliot's avowed project as a novelist to present 'mixed human beings in such a way as to call forth tolerant judgement, pity and sympathy' (*Letters*, II, 299). 'Tolerant' is the important word here: the language that created George Eliot's characters was appealing to and trying to foster a mindset that could tolerate the difficulty of thinking and feeling possibly contradictory thoughts and emotions. If emotional identification always needs the corrective of judgement in relation to, for instance, Dorothea's absurd idealization of Mr Casaubon as the highest type of father-husband, then judgement is exposed as unimaginative and premature, reductive and obtuse in the absence of sympathetic understanding. Increasingly in the early chapters the anonymous provincial and practical voices of the opening chapter are embodied in distinct flesh and blood characters who represent ordinary and conventional wisdom: so Sir James (Dorothea's suitor) in Chapter 2 believes that Dorothea's 'excessive religiousness' will 'die out with marriage' (21); while for Mrs Cadwallader in Chapter 6 it is 'a great deal of nonsense . . . a flighty sort of Methodistical stuff' (56). The temptation to patronize Dorothea is constantly checked by its attitudinal overlap with the provincial narrowness and prejudice represented in these judgments, while the cumulative effect of the same is to make the reader sympathetically aware of the circumscribed social world in which Dorothea must seek to satisfy her lofty desires, and, at some level, to vindicate her mistake in believing that Casaubon can offer what commonplace Middlemarch life cannot. 'The *fad* of drawing plans!' thinks Dorothea, when Celia has thus dismissively spoken of Dorothea's philanthropic scheme for housing the estate's labourers: 'What was life worth – what great faith was possible when the whole effect of one's actions could be withered up into such parched rubbish as that?' (36). The impersonal magnitude of these questions, even their self-consciously elevated language, seems contextually to work free of the incipient irony of the sentence because they are true signs of something more than merely personal or emotional in Dorothea. 'What was life worth?', only mutedly ironized here, is the central, essentially religious question begged by every major character and narrative in this book.

One of the subtle achievements of George Eliot's use of free indirect mode at such times is to suggest that the truest response might lie elusively *between* the conventional categories of true and false, right and wrong: 'Wrong reasoning sometimes lands poor mortals in right conclusions: starting a long way off the true point, and proceeding by loops and zig-zags, we now and then arrive just where we ought to be' (25). As Derek Oldfield suggests, in his important study of the language of the novel, this effectively describes George Eliot's method in *Middlemarch*:

> Instead of telling us directly what to think, George Eliot frequently just tells us what we may *not* think – or lets us oscillate between one attitude which needs qualifying and another. This modifying process [amounts to] a succession of probes at the truth . . . The reader has to respond to the text with the closest possible attention if s/he is to react accurately to the multiple points of view including Dorothea's own distorted view of herself. (See Hardy, 1967, 67)

The novel 'zig-zags' between (partial) points of view in relation to each character, moving more or less gradually, from distant sweep to close-up view, and thus keeping the reader morally, mentally and imaginatively alert, and unable to settle complacently into uncritical acceptance of one single view. 'There must be a systole and diastole in all inquiry,' the doctor Lydgate is quoted as saying: 'a man's mind must be continually expanding and shrinking between the whole human horizon and the horizon of an object-glass' (630). Just so, this novel is a 'complex perspectival system [in which] perspectives multiply and balance':

> Around one centre of interest and attention and then the next, and the next, shifting constellations of viewpoint gather and dissolve . . . The narrative slide from one view to the other engages readers in a kind of suspense that has little to do with plot.[5]

Casaubon

The unsettling effect of the novel's unique kind of suspense is particularly strong in relation to Mr Casaubon, whom an inward view is withheld until Chapter 10, as if to highlight the moral imperative of the novel's method. For, as the narrator makes explicit, in ordinary life the ego has no space for an expansive perspective that can see and feel more than one thing at once in relation to other human beings:

> I protest against any absolute conclusion, any prejudice derived from Mrs Cadwallader's contempt . . . Sir James Chettam's poor opinion . . . or from Celia's criticism. Suppose we turn from outside estimates of a man, to wonder, with keener interest, what is the report of his own consciousness about his doings or capacity . . . Doubtless his lot is important in his own eyes; and the chief reason that we think he asks too large a place in our consideration must be our want of room for him . . . (82)

When George Steiner described *Middlemarch* as the most 'strenuously narrated' novel in English, he had in mind this 'personal interference' (as he termed it disparagingly) where 'George Eliot attempts to persuade us of what should be artistically evident'.[6] This common objection to George Eliot's fictional mode is partly a matter of aesthetic taste. The tradition of the omniscient or all-knowing author convention and of the intrusive narrator fell out of favour in the last century. In an age of increasing scepticism, modern readers were (and are) reluctant to accept the sort of God-like authority assumed by the omniscient narrator, and more likely to be at home with the Jamesian dictum of 'showing not telling' and with the modernist ideal of impersonality.[7] Towards the close of the last century George Eliot's over-dominant presence in her novels was attacked from a number of literary-theoretical positions. Her moralizing, didactic voice was accused of placing the author and reader in an illegitimate position of superiority with regard to the stories and characters depicted. The author-narrator and reader, who is in possession of the author's specialized wisdom, always knows more and always knows better than the characters, who are explained definitively from the outside.[8]

Yet George Eliot's narratorial interventions are as varied and textured as her use of free indirect mode, and rarely as redundant or as merely external to character as these generalized criticisms suggest. So in Chapter 10, when the narration 'turns' from those 'outward estimates' of Casaubon – 'no better than a mummy', 'a great bladder for dried peas to rattle in' (56–7) – to the report of Casaubon's own consciousness as his marriage to Dorothea approaches:

> In truth, as the day fixed for his marriage came nearer, Mr Casaubon did not find his spirits rising; nor did the contemplation of that matrimonial garden-scene, where, as all experience showed, the path was to be bordered with flowers, prove persistently more enchanting to him than the accustomed vaults where he walked taper in hand. He did not confess to himself, still less could he have breathed to another, his surprise that though he had won a lovely and noble-hearted girl he had not won delight – which he had also regarded as an object to be found by search . . .
>
> Poor Mr Casaubon had imagined that his long studious bachelorhood had stored up for him a compound interest of enjoyment, and that large drafts on his affections would not fail to be honoured . . . And now he was in danger of being saddened by the very conviction that his circumstances were unusually happy: there was nothing external by which he could account for a certain blankness of sensibility which came over him just when his expectant gladness should have been most lively, just when he exchanged the accustomed dullness of his Lowick library for his visits to the Grange. Here was a weary experience in which he was as utterly condemned to loneliness as in the despair which sometimes threatened him while toiling in the morass of authorship without seeming nearer to the goal. And his was that worst loneliness which would shrink from pity. (83)

Despite the protective tenderness of 'Poor Mr Casaubon' and the mediating narratorial sympathy, the first paragraph of this extract often adopts the content and cadence of Casaubon's thought only to turn it against him. His inward ruminations on marriage have all the formality and the ring of 'a public statement' (17) that his very first speech in the novel is described as having, as well as the detached, externalized sentiment that makes his debut as a lover – his letter of proposal to Dorothea in Chapter 5 – so chilling. The mix of studiedly high-flown poetic clichés – the 'matrimonial garden-scene' whose path is to be 'bordered with flowers' – with his usual formal precision – the 'compound interest of enjoyment' which he imagines to be owing to him as a result of his long bachelorhood – is disturbing as well as faintly comic, not simply because the subject here is personal need, feeling, human relations and love, but because this externalized mode is presented as constituting – or substituting for – Casaubon's inner life.

Thus, there is an element of tact or 'decorum'[9] in the narration's relatively sparing or incomplete use of free indirect mode in the move to the next paragraph. It is difficult to encourage emotional identification with a character whose distinguishing feature is presented here as a lack of emotion. Closer inward contact with this mind or mode could only alienate sympathy and compound criticism, by revealing more intimately that this emotional lack is one which Casaubon himself has not feeling enough to experience as a lack. Hence, he looks elsewhere – to something 'external . . . [to] account for [his] blankness of sensibility', like the 'mummy' or 'great bladder' Middlemarch says he is. The point of the narrator's corrective estimate is to insist that those aspects of Casaubon which make him all the less attractive as a husband for Dorothea – his incapacity for feeling (and sexual impotence perhaps?) and his lack of an inner life – make him all the more to be pitied as a man. This explains why George Eliot as narrator feels compelled so often in the course of the novel to speak on Casaubon's behalf – to say *for* him what he cannot say for himself. The author intervenes at such times in the role of narrator to make up for her character's deficiencies. A person like Casaubon cannot or dares not detail their weaknesses to themselves let alone anyone else: 'He did not confess to himself, still less could he have breathed to another . . .' George Eliot is, at such times, an added extra because she provides in her novel the voice so often lacking in actual life that speaks up for the failed or inadequate life and saves it, if only at the level of verbal recognition, from being merely failure.

Bulstrode

The final example of this section shows how the verbal resources under discussion here work together when the author is at her most psychologically subtle. Mr Bulstrode is George Eliot's most Hardyesque figure – a man who finds himself involuntarily and ironically pursued and dogged by the past life he had hoped to have long left behind. Late in the novel, he finds himself in the position of nursing the sick Raffles (Bulstrode's former accomplice in his dubious business practices, who is now blackmailing him), with strict instructions from Lydgate as to his treatment. In the dead of night, Bulstrode is keeping watch over his patient:

> Whatever prayers he might lift up, whatever statements he might inwardly make of this man's wretched spiritual condition, and the duty he himself was under to submit to the punishment divinely appointed for him rather than to wish for evil to another – through all this effort to condense words into a solid mental state, there pierced and spread with irresistible vividness the images of the events he desired. And in the train of these images came their apology. He could not but see the death of Raffles, and see in it his own deliverance. What was the removal of this wretched creature? He was impenitent – but were not public criminals impenitent? – yet the law decided on their fate. Should Providence in this case award death, there was no sin in contemplating death as the desirable issue – if he kept his hands from hastening it – if he scrupulously did what was prescribed. Even here there might be a mistake; human prescriptions were fallible things: Lydgate had said that treatment had hastened death, – why not his own method of treatment? But of course intention was everything in the question of right and wrong. (692–3)

Free indirect mode emerges (decorously) here at the point where Bulstrode has committed himself to the 'old Adam' (171) within: 'What was the removal of this wretched creature?' is an internalized version of the devil's own voice. The grand narrative of sin and temptation thus taking place in a subterranean realm helps explain the inception of the psychological novel; and the narrator's language here is at first committed to the minute unfolding of the process by which evil replaces good.

But this is also a moment at which language has become redundant at one level. For what makes temptation so powerful here is the fact that desire is experienced not as thought, idea or word but as something more primary – as an image or perception: 'He could not but *see* the death of Raffles . . .'; 'there spread with irresistible vividness the *images* of the events he desired'. George Eliot's language and endeavour at such times is closely analogous to Lydgate's scientific pursuits in biology to 'reveal subtle actions inaccessible by any sort of lens, but tracked in that outer darkness through long pathways of necessary sequence':[10]

He wanted to pierce the obscurity of those minute processes which prepare human misery and joy, those invisible thoroughfares which are the first lurking-places of anguish, mania, and crime, that delicate poise and transition which determine the growth of happy or unhappy consciousness. (163)

Yet the 'scientific' endeavour is never morally neutral in *Middlemarch*. The invisible lurking-place where Bulstrode sees 'his own deliverance' is the equivalent in this novel to the moment of the Fall. Its immediate moral consequence is disclosed in the subsequent knock-on sentence: 'In the train of those images came their apology.' As soon as the desired end dictates the decision, so soon does Bulstrode have to banish the moral thinking part of himself, and even put reason distortedly in the service of the realization of his desire: 'Should Providence in this case award death, there was no sin in contemplating death as the desirable issue . . . Even here there might be a mistake; human prescriptions were fallible things.' When Bulstrode's reasoning faculty is thus used to justify his own wrong-doing he has effectively jettisoned the critical intelligence that could prevent that wrongdoing. And almost as immediately that critical intelligence comes retributively back, in those 'yet', 'if' and 'but' clauses which ensue: 'Yet the law decided . . .'; 'if he scrupulously did what was prescribed'; 'But of course intention was everything . . .' The complexity exists not for its own sake here but to register with minute exactitude the subtle actions of the (morally distorting) thinking mind in time.

George Eliot was at times compelled to justify the inclusiveness of her writing style, and its abundance of second thoughts. 'I am unable to alter anything in relation to the delineation or development of character', she told her publisher at the beginning of her writing

career, 'as my stories always grow out of my psychological conception of the dramatis personae' (*Letters*, ii, 299). The richness and
eclecticism of the discourses of *Middlemarch* – religious, literary,
artistic, psychological, philosophical – is paradoxically the result,
it seems, of language always having secondary status for George
Eliot as an expressive vehicle for prior conception. To that degree,
the inclusiveness of the novel is the outcome of her pragmatic
approach to probing the truth: anything and everything might serve
if it can. Yet in paragraphs like the above, the very precision of the
language gives it the status of a kind of mental primary 'tissue' (147):
as George Eliot's supreme moral stamina imaginatively inhabits the
invisible thoroughfares of Bulstrode's mind, what emerges in that
'Yet . . . if . . . if . . . but' sequence is the very syntax of moral
conflict, the deep grammar of inwardly avenging conscience.

But this is a witnessing as well as a relating presence. Bulstrode
cannot admit these second thoughts to himself and still go on with
the action he contemplates. Thus, the thoughts which he will not
have or own, the reasoning and critical consciousness which he ban-
ishes, George Eliot's voice recaptures in the succeeding paragraph:

> And Bulstrode set himself to keep his intentions separate from his
> desire. He inwardly declared that he intended to obey orders. Why
> should he have got into any argument about the validity of these
> orders? It was only the common trick of desire – which avails
> itself of any irrelevant scepticism, finding larger room for itself in
> all uncertainty about effects, in every obscurity that looks like the
> absence of law. (693)

Bulstrode is using the apparent lack of imperative to do one thing,
or another – whatever 'looks like an absence of law' – to do what he
wants to do. George Eliot is famously reported as having said in relation to the three concepts of 'God, Immortality, Duty, 'how incon-
ceivable was the *first*, how unbelievable the *second*, and yet how
peremptory and absolute the *third*' (Ashton, 1996, 333). Bulstrode
is himself half-conscious of eschewing that absolute law. Thus, when
George Eliot stands in as a reminder of duty here, she is not so much
explaining Bulstrode *for* him. Rather, she is articulating thoughts
which originate in Bulstrode but which he himself is refusing to
own or embody. Indeed it is because George Eliot believed (after
Feuerbach) in the inward life as the higher law that she feels obliged

to commit to language the inward condition of people who refuse to do so for themselves. Language at such times operates as a secular replacement for a lost divinity. Its business used to belong to God: judging, forgiving, extenuating or affirming those actions for which there may well be no visible reward or punishment in merely human terms. The voice and language we call 'George Eliot' is thus, in part, a creation of Feuerbachian principles. It speaks in memory of those virtues and values which the author feared were being lost with the loss of formal Christianity, even as that form was humanly created.

THE NOVEL'S FORM

Structure

Middlemarch is the product of the blending of two separately conceived stories, that of 'Miss Brooke', conceived as a short tale, and that of a study of provincial society, entitled *Middlemarch*, centring on Lydgate. This section will show how the initial melding together of distinct stories set the pattern for the novel as a whole, as it expanded to include the complexly inter-related stories of Fred, Mary and the Garths, and of the Bulstrodes. Yet the degree to which the separate integrity of these stories is to a large extent preserved is immediately indicated by the structure of the first two books: 'Miss Brooke' came to form the Prelude and the first nine to ten chapters of the completed novel; the original *Middlemarch* became the basis of Chapters 11 to 16.

The impression of moving through sequences of stories, each with their own plot-lines, start and end points, and even generic definitions – comic pastoral in the case of Fred and Mary, sensation fiction in the case of the Bulstrode-Raffles story – is emphasized and in part determined by the novel's mode of publication. Originally published in eight separate instalments, each substantial part or 'book' has its own separate title and is like a little novel in itself. The first reading audience received each book at roughly two-monthly intervals, thus sharing over 18 months a novel that covered three years. The writing and reading experience is as gradually progressive as the stories themselves (and takes approximately the same length of time). Moreover, read this way, the novel offers a continuous experience of beginnings and endings (which are never artificially climactic or suspenseful) that is consonant with the vision of life, as a rhythmically repetitive series of openings and closures, expressed in the opening sentence of the Finale: 'Every limit is a beginning as well as an ending' (815). *Middlemarch* is characteristically concerned with life as a progress through significant epochs, and this sense of life as a journey with crucial staging posts is reinforced by the publication convention.

The several linear narratives are nonetheless knitted together, at the level of character and plot, with quietly scrupulous care and intricacy. Chapters 10 and 17, as we shall see more fully in the remainder of this chapter, are pivotal in this regard, respectively bringing together Dorothea and Lydgate, and Lydgate and Farebrother, while, in the latter instance, deftly introducing Farebrother's relationship to the Garths on the one hand ('There's a parishioner of mine – a fine fellow, but who would hardly have pulled through as he has done without his wife. Do you know the Garths?' (172)), and to Bulstrode on the other. Thus the novel's forward movement also rounds out, as if connecting up hitherto invisible dots, the network of associations (Bulstrode–Vincy–Featherstone) that have already come to form the social milieu in which Lydgate will seek to realize his scientific and professional ambitions. Lydgate, in fact, appears at all the Middlemarch locations in Books One and Two (Tipton Grange, the Vincys', the bank, Stone Court), and in Book Three the respective illnesses at Stone Court, the Vincys' and Lowick Manor ensure that Lydgate, in his professional role as doctor, remains the narrative link between the various groupings as well as between the gentry (Casaubons) and the bourgeoisie (Vincys). The ground is very carefully prepared at the close of Chapter 27 for Lydgate's appearance at Lowick Manor in Chapters 29 and 30: detailing Lydgate's guarded pleasure at 'inspiriting signs' of his gradual acceptance as a professional in the neighbourhood, the concluding paragraph mentions, seemingly *en passant*, that 'only a few days later . . . when he had happened to overtake Rosamond on the Lowick road . . . he had been stopped by a servant on horseback with a message calling him to a house of some importance' (270). George Eliot's attention to 'joining' devices of this kind ensure that the narrative moves seamlessly, and apparently casually, from one story or social grouping to another.

Moreover, aside from the first book, which is dedicated almost entirely to Dorothea's story, all subsequent books have titles that explicitly draw attention to points of connection across the individual story strands. The title of Book Two, 'Old and Young', not only reflects the contrast between youth and age in the several stories (Fred Vincy and his uncle Featherstone; Dorothea and Casaubon; Lydgate and Bulstrode; Fred Vincy and Bulstrode; Will and Casaubon): it also alerts us to the further parallels between these stories insofar as each representative of the younger generation is dependent upon their elder counterpart for financial support either in furthering their respective ambitions (in the case of Lydgate and Will, and even Dorothea), or merely (in the case of Fred) in staying solvent. At the same time, it emerges that the elders have little to offer the young in other respects: Featherstone, Bulstrode and Casaubon are no less self-absorbed or subject to egoistic illusions than their youthful protégés and, in fact, the moral authority tends to rest with the latter, insofar as their egoistic drives are directed towards altruistic ends.

These emerging parallels and contrasts are enriched by the immediately succeeding books. The title of Book Two, 'Waiting for Death', bears simultaneous reference to two sick men and their mourners-in-waiting: Fred is waiting for Featherstone's death to deliver him from debt and from the obligation to make a decision about what to do with his life, and Mary too (more literally since she is nursing the sick man) is waiting for the event that will also determine her own future (as Fred's wife or, alternatively, as a teacher or governess). After her conversation with Lydgate in Chapter 30, Dorothea also begins to wait for husband's death (and Mrs Vincy in Chapter 26 might also be said to be waiting for Fred's death, though his illness turns out not to be fatal). The explicit attention drawn to such correspondences by each book title – 'Three Love Problems', 'The Widow and the Wife', 'Two Temptations', and so on – puts the reader in the habit of seeing more subtle and potentially more far-reaching resemblances. Two of the most important parallels of Book Three, for instance, are signalled unassertively by the juxtaposition of Chapters 32 and 33, where the greedy opportunism of the Featherstone 'hangers-on' is implicitly contrasted with Mary's acceptance that 'things were not likely to be arranged for her peculiar satisfaction' (311). Likewise, in Chapters 30 and 31 Dorothea's generous selflessness in relation to Casaubon's needs is suggestively positioned back-to-back with Rosamond's narrow egoism and the danger it spells for Lydgate, as the two marriages are increasingly delineated in ironical resemblance and difference to one another.

Moreover, the title of Book Three seems to be establishing a parallel that will become more important *after* the deaths of Casaubon and Featherstone, such is the cumulative resonance of this novel. 'The Dead Hand' – the title of Book Five – refers directly to Casaubon and the instructions contained in his will (which effectively prevent Dorothea's marriage to Ladislaw), yet it also echoes a phrase used in relation to Featherstone in Chapter 34: 'In chuckling over the vexations he could inflict by the rigid clutch of his dead hand, he inevitably mingled his consciousness with that lived stagnant presence, and so far as he was preoccupied with a future life, it was one of gratification inside his coffin' (320). The egoistic bondage even of Featherstone's imagined afterlife resonates retrospectively with Casaubon's 'fenced in sensibilities' (278), the 'dark closet' (277) of his mind, and the narrow sensitive jealousy which is 'a blight bred in the cloudy, damp despondency of uneasy egoism' (208). As Barbara Hardy has pointed out, the Featherstone episodes are 'a grotesque comedy acting as a kind of distorting mirror of the story of Dorothea and Casaubon' (Hardy [1959], 122). Yet, while the author's notebooks to the novel indicate that the connection between the Featherstone and Casaubon wills was an intended one, the link is not made explicitly. Rather, the very unforced, loose, inexact nature of the correspondence richly yields further possible correspondences and connections which may or not be picked up by the reader. For instance: 'the dead hand of Featherstone or Casaubon paradoxically liberates and re-vivifies those whom it was meant to govern and thwart; Bulstrode's past, which he thought dead and buried, springs to life and destroys him' (Harvey, 145)

As the remainder of this chapter and the next will show, *Middlemarch* abounds in symmetries and echoes, antitheses and parallels, which are held in delicately mobile balance and implicit counterpoint. The formal patterning is rendered largely invisible by the engrossing realist interest and power of the ordinary human lives depicted, even as that very power partly gathers its force from the rich analogies and doublings that formally surround each separate instance or story. Thus, on the one hand, the novel's blueprint of formal strictness generously helps to create a multiplicity of layers of meaning or significance. On the other, this formal organization, while neither stiffly nor strictly determined, nonetheless holds together and concentrates the implications of the novel's expansive mass of life. Collectively and undogmatically, the form describes (as a circle describes itself) implicit moral arguments or generalizations.

Imagery

Perhaps the clearest way of demonstrating this binding yet open-ended formal pattern is through the novel's imagery. Often apparently casual images form part of an intricate composition, cluster or chain of images, which formally connect and distinguish the diverse narratives and protagonists. Frustrated ambition, for instance, generates a train of images that are freely and fluidly exchanged between characters. When 'Miss Brooke' finds herself transformed into Mrs Casaubon in Rome, she feels 'with a stifling depression that the large vistas and wide fresh air which she had dreamed of finding in her husband's mind were replaced by ante-rooms and winding passages which seemed to lead nowither' (193); 'She was gradually ceasing to expect with her former delightful confidence that she should see any wide opening where she followed him. Poor Mr Casaubon himself was lost among small closets and winding stairs' (195). Dorothea's experience of narrowness, confinement and enclosure implicitly cues the reader to recall the occurrence of such language in the early chapters of the novel, where we see her 'struggling in the bonds of a narrow teaching, hemmed in by a social life which seemed nothing but a labyrinth of petty courses, a walled-in maze of small paths that led no whither' (28). The imagery which at first attached to Dorothea's predicament as a single woman now attaches to her situation as wife.

The terrible irony that she has escaped nothing, and only exchanged one form of imprisonment for another and more permanent one, is nonetheless presented unobtrusively rather than heavily underscored, partly because the imagery of enclosure and confinement in Chapters 19 to 21 is so well supported by and appropriately borrowed from the literal context. The figurative 'ante-rooms and winding passages' of Casaubon's mind, for instance, have literal existence in the Vatican library where Casaubon carries out his research. The novel habitually makes metaphorical use of elements physically present within it. Images are picked up from Casaubon's antiquarian researches, from his 'plodding' (81) method of work and from the locales in which he studies. At Lowick too he is associated with the heavy-shuttered library and the small-windowed side of the house, where Dorothea occupies the blue-green boudoir (and window), the significance of which in the image patterns of the novel is discussed in Chapter 3. Moreover, it can be difficult to know where, if at all, literal objects or scenes or facts turn into figurative ones: 'With his taper stuck before him,' we are told of Casaubon, 'he forgot the absence of windows, and in bitter manuscript remarks on other men's notions about the solar deities, he had become indifferent to the sunlight' (195). The 'absence of windows' and 'indifference to sunlight' seem both real *and* suggestively symbolic of the stultifying imprisonment of Casaubon's mind and ego as Dorothea experiences it, just as the contrasting 'gush of inward light illuminating the transparent skin as well as the eyes' (202–3) when Will Ladislaw smiles has a physical reality.

A further real and powerful presence that takes on a symbolic dimension in these chapters are of course the ruins of Rome, which have a different significance in the delineation of these three characters. In Dorothea's case the ruins externalize symbolically, even as they help to create, her mental and moral perturbation. For Will, by contrast, they offer creative opportunity: 'the fragments stimulated his imagination and made him constructive' (209). On Casaubon, they make no impact personally: the gigantic broken revelations of Rome, which offer so powerfully suggestive a correlative to the futility of Casaubon's search for a 'key to all mythologies', are outside the scope of his imagination. Moreover, in Casaubon's case the ruins are a literal, concrete version of a train of association that began in Chapter 2 to suggest the moribund uselessness of Casaubon's work. In Chapter 2, Casaubon speaks of his own mind as 'something like the ghost of an ancient, wandering about the world and trying mentally to construct it as it used to be, in spite of ruin and confusing changes' (17). In Chapter 10, Ladislaw is contemptuous of Casaubon's 'learned theory exploring the tossed ruins of the world' (81). Right up until the moment of his death, Casaubon's work is characterized in relation to 'shattered mummies' and 'crushed ruins' (472). Where literal objects helped to produce the imagery of confinement, in this case they confirm, ratify and concretize existing image clusters. The use of the ruins of Rome as a symbol that has a range of related significances – and which shifts from one meaning to another as the symbol is brought into relationship with different characters – is a clue to the way in which images typically operate in this novel. They are simultaneously embedded in the narrative and almost Shakespearean in their reach and influence through the work as a whole.

Inclusiveness

At the opening of Chapter 19, Dorothea is espied by Will Ladislaw and his artist friend Naumann as she stands close to a sculpture of the reclining Ariadne in the Vatican, 'not looking at the sculpture, probably not thinking of it: her large eyes were fixed dreamily on a streak of sunlight which fell across the floor':

> 'What do you think of that for a fine bit of antithesis?' said the German . . . 'There lies antique beauty, not corpse-like even in death, but arrested in the complete contentment of its sensuous perfection: and here stands beauty in its breathing life, with the consciousness of Christian centuries in its bosom. But she should be dressed as a nun.'(187)

Naumann's interpretation of Dorothea as a work of art invites an emblematic reading of this scene. Dorothea, 'a breathing blooming girl, whose form is not shamed by the Aridane', nevertheless is turned away from that expression of sensual contentment, as if reluctant to recognize the sensuous power within herself which the voluptuous Ariadne here represents.[11] The novel creates a further (structural) antithesis when, at the close of Chapter 20, we see the same scene now from Dorothea's inward view:

> She did not really see the streak of sunlight on the floor more than she saw the statues: she was inwardly seeing the light of years to come in her own home and over the English fields and elms . . . and feeling that the way in which they might be filled with joyful devotedness was not so clear as it had been. (200)

The Dorothea whom Naumann has aesthetically placed amidst Rome's antique classical forms feels no sense of relation to her immediate environment except (as the opening of Chapter 20 illustrates) of a disorientatingly alienating kind. Moreover, Naumann's aestheticizing response to Dorothea externally fixes her in a determining attitude at the very moment when, inwardly, she is experiencing the most tumultuous change. The close and careful dovetailing of these interpretatively contrasting scenes demonstrates one of the principal structural characteristics of this novel. Its design is scrupulously calculated so as to render interpretation and meaning as 'incalculable' and 'diffuse' (see 822) as possible. The indeterminacy is not, as this section will show, a symptom of the author's scepticism in relation to meaning, but an indication of how a moral-aesthetic distrust of selective vision determined the form of *Middlemarch*, as we have seen it influencing the novel's language.

Perspective and Scale

The close of Book One shows how George Eliot made a virtue of the technical problem of uniting the two projects.[12] Halfway through Chapter 10 of *Middlemarch*, following the account of the first disagreement between Dorothea and Casaubon, the narration shifts suddenly from internal identification with the 'real hurt' Dorothea suffers to an externalized and dramatic appreciation: 'She recovered her equanimity, and was an agreeable image of serene dignity when she came into the drawing-room in her silver-grey dress' (86). Here, the shift from inward to outward estimate occurs deftly and within just one sentence, so that by the opening of the following paragraph we find ourselves already beginning to see Dorothea through the eyes of the professional (male) company gathered for dinner, mayor and manufacturer, banker, lawyer, doctor: ' "A fine woman, Miss Brooke!, an uncommonly fine woman, by God!" said Mr Standish, the old lawyer' (87). Within the space of two paragraphs the focus has shifted away from intense and concentrated interest in Dorothea and immersed the reader in the society and gossip of Middlemarch life. When the narrative focuses again on Dorothea she is of interest not simply for her own sake but because she is in 'animated conversation' with the interesting newcomer and medical man Mr Lydgate. The ultimate point of this chapter is to shift the narrative's centre of interest away from Dorothea to Lydgate, but the immediate effect of the chapter is not a simple switch of focus from one character to another but a sudden expansion of interest. Up to this point *Middlemarch* has begun to give the story the Prelude promised: that of a woman, a latter-day St Theresa, whose idealistic ambitions and potentialities for ardent and heroic enterprise are frustrated by the double limitations of her sex and the social conditions of the age. This chapter is presenting Middlemarch the place, offering 'a microcosm of Middlemarch society . . . in dramatic form . . . [to] give solidity and extension to the protagonists we already know' (Harvey, 129), and thus fulfilling the expectations offered by the novel's full title: *Middlemarch: A Study of Provincial Life*.

Yet Gillian Beer has pointed out the importance of distinguishing between *Middlemarch* the book and Middlemarch the town:

> The inhabitants of Middlemarch within the book are so confident that Middlemarch is not only in the Midlands but in the Middle of the world; the book's expansiveness creates an effect of size for the town, so that Paris, Rome and London look thin and small by comparison . . . The narrator's business is to remind us of worlds intellectual, aesthetic, spiritual, which do not naturally flourish in the provinces. Not only the individual selves but the collective social self of Middlemarch is framed and placed. (1983, 173)

While Middlemarchers may feel they occupy the Middle of the world, the novel, in its very title, draws attention to their middling mediocrity, their essential typicality and ordinariness. And formally, too, the novel continually manipulates this expansion and contraction of scale. For so soon as Dorothea is thus socially placed, rounded and extended at one level, simultaneously the importance of her individual story begins to diminish. What had begun by seeming to be merely substantiating background to the Dorothea-Casaubon story, now becomes foreground: it is the Middlemarchers themselves (the Bulstrodes, the Vincys) who will be taking centre stage over the next eight chapters or so. The diminishment is an implicit vindication of the Prelude's pronouncements on the impossibility of exceptional action in a fallen world. As Barbara Hardy has pointed out, 'Dorothea cannot be a Saint Theresa in this society': and the problem she thus represents 'must be developed without one engrossing figure' (1959, 94).

So the novel now hands the baton to Lydgate and his ambition 'to do good small work for Middlemarch, and great work for the world' (147). Within a few chapters, in another sleight-of-scale, the smallness of Middlemarch, which at first offers itself to Lydgate as a virtue – 'he was not going to have his vanities provoked by contact with the showy worldly successes of the capital, but to live among people who could hold no rivalry with that pursuit of a great idea' (145) – threatens to defeat his purposes through the irresistible might of its very pettiness. Compelled for pragmatic reasons to vote with Mr Bulstrode's choice for the hospital chaplaincy (and thus against Mr Farebrother, whom his instinct prefers), he 'for the first time . . .

was feeling the hampering threadlike pressure of small social conditions, and their frustrating complexity'(178). Moreover, the kind of
readjustment of worldview that the story here presses upon Lydgate
is, in the course of this same episode, forced upon the reader at the
level of the narrative,[13] with the introduction of Mr Farebrother
in person in Chapter 17. The reader's first impressions of Mr
Farebrother are mediated through Lydgate's immediately favourable
perception – 'He came like a pleasant change in the light . . . His
face . . . was a striking mixture of the shrewd and the mild' (159–61)
– which at first seems merely correctively to balance Bulstrode's
earlier unfavourable estimate of Farebrother as 'a man deeply
painful to contemplate' (124). The good opinion Lydgate has
formed of his new acquaintance now influences the reader's
response to Mr Farebrother's half-heartedness and disappointment
in respect of his vocation in a way utterly contrary to Bulstrode's:
'The Vicar's frankness seemed not of the repulsive sort that comes
from an uneasy consciousness seeking to forestall the judgement of
others, but simply the relief of a desire to do with as little pretence
as possible' (170). In the dialogue between the two men this quality
of authenticity in Farebrother's character begins to have currency in
its own right and to live apart from Lydgate's perceptions to the
degree that, increasingly, the reader is inclined to view Lydgate and
his predicament through the wisdom, experience and percipience of
Farebrother's view, especially when he comments on the difficulties
involved in Lydgate's scheme to reform the medical profession from
within: 'You have not only got the old Adam in yourself against you,
but you have got all those descendants of the original Adam who
form the society around you' (171).

This is another illustration, of course, of the perspectival complexity we saw earlier in this chapter, and is an example too of the
ways in which the novel dramatizes the process by which 'character'
is shaped, by making 'the reciprocal workings of self-regard and
opinion primary':

> [The novel] enforces the fact that in dealing with a particular
> person we must consider: his appearance in the eyes of each of
> the other persons he encounters; the way he appears among
> various social groupings to which he is known or which know of
> him; and his own complex of feelings which leads him to offer the
> world a version (or various versions) of himself (sic).[14]

Later deconstructive interpretations of the novel have suggested that 'character' in *Middlemarch* is presented as itself a kind of 'fiction', 'a matter of illusion and misconstruction':

> Characters are constantly misreading the signs they see in each other and constructing illusory portraits which are the product of their own desires. The inhabitants of *Middlemarch* are also shown to construct illusory images of themselves, repressing what they refuse to recognise as part of their psychological make-up . . . The novel gives explicit recognition to the process by which our conception of character is constructed, the way in which a coherent image both of the self and of others is built . . . [It] recognises that all understanding of personality is a construction analogous to the process of reading a character. (Wright, 39–50)

But the effect inside the life of the novel of these shifts of perspective is more radical than even an implicitly (and pre-emptive) 'post-modern' theory of character might be. For it is never simply the case that we are introduced to an alternative or competing 'point of view'. Rather, it is as if we enter a new world, an entirely separate, self-governing system or 'constellation': 'What seems a casual shift of attention,' says Elizabeth Deeds Ermarth, 'turns out to be mountainous travel to an entirely different corner of the cosmos' (Chase, 2006, 123). For Mr Farebrother's and Lydgate's worldviews cannot be incorporated into one another, as the close of Chapter 18 makes clear. After the chaplaincy election, Mr Farebrother meets Lydgate 'with the same friendliness as before', while Lydgate thinks there is 'a pitiable infirmity of will in Mr Farebrother' when the latter tells him 'I am not a mighty man – I shall never be a man of renown' (185). In the preceding paragraph the narrator has summed up the paradox that Mr Farebrother represents: 'by dint of admitting to himself that he was too much as other men were, he had become remarkably unlike them in this – that he could excuse others for thinking slightly of him, and could judge impartially of their conduct even when it told against him' (ibid.). Farebrother's modesty is his might, yet that might depends upon his *not* being able to see his virtue as the narrator can; while Lydgate's talents absolutely require bold self-recognition if they are to have any hope of being realized in the world. These systems are as incommensurate as they are stubbornly resistant to invalidation one by the other. The wonder is that they exist, thus cordially, together in the same world.

Exhibiting the plurality of worlds, as we shall see at the close of this chapter, is what the realist novel does best. But in *Middlemarch* the phenomenon occurs with an unusual degree of consciousness of its moral and metaphysical implications, and with an unrelenting purpose of putting both reader and character in possession of those implications. Thus when, after Dorothea's struggles have filled our consciousness almost exclusively in the first nine chapters of the novel, the reader now has to recognize that she is just one interest among many others, the reader is finding out what Dorothea herself has to recognize in the course of the novel, and with an approximation to the same kind of seismic reorientation. While yet on honeymoon with Mr Casaubon, she 'felt the waking of a presentiment that there might be a sad consciousness in his life which made as great a need on his side as on her own':

> We are all of us born in moral stupidity, taking the world as an udder to feed our supreme selves: Dorothea had early begun to emerge from that stupidity, but yet it had been easier to her to imagine how she would devote herself to Mr Casaubon, and become wise and strong in his strength and wisdom, than to conceive with that distinctness which is no longer reflection but feeling – an idea wrought back to the directness of sense, like the solidity of objects – that he had an equivalent centre of self, whence the lights and shadows must always fall with a certain difference. (208)

As we shall see in the next chapter, this moment is as lonely as it is morally enlarging, and a loss as much as gain, for in the recognition of their shared equivalence there is a recognition too that, together in marriage, the couple are mutually sundered. Moreover, even this decisive recognition of multiplicity is multiply aspected, with its 'reflective' and its 'sensory' side. For Spinoza, mind and body were not separate but parallel realms, aspects of one another. The capacity for the kind of translation recorded in Dorothea here from mind to body, idea to sensation, thought to feeling, is at the heart of his ethical philosophy in ways that are crucial, as we shall see, to George Eliot's vision in Book Eight of the novel, but critical also to her moral project in writing the novel. For all their intellectualism,

George Eliot did not want her books to end in ideas but to be activated in the world, like a secular form of the word made flesh.

For Gillian Beer this activation of the reader's 'primary perception' is a function of the novel's imagery. Metaphor 'releases' in the reader 'lateral connections': it 'disturbs stereotypes and the fixity of natural law' by richly condensing multiple meanings and by the 'unforeseen discharge of new affinity':

> Fugitive kinship is discovered in metaphor: affinity proves to be real without needing to be permanent. George Eliot's . . . intensely metaphoric style offers multiple routes beyond the world of *Middlemarch* itself, discovering at once connection and difference . . . making space for divergence and possibility. In the act of realising metaphor [the reader] repeats the ideal activity enjoined by the book' – that of 'making connections.' (Beer, 1986, 192–3)

Thus, the dominant and diffuse web imagery that is woven into the novel's language is as much an image of the operation of metaphor itself in the novel as it is ubiquitously the 'textural counterpart' of the novel's structure (Harvey, 241).[15] In place of the exclusive history of one human lot (as in the Victorian *Bildungsroman*), *Middlemarch* offers a whole network of overlapping character groupings and centres of activity and interest, all of which become so enmeshed and interwoven that it is impossible to follow one thread in the story of a single life without coming upon the various other threads which cross, intercept or frustrate it. Combined with the novel's constant rotation of interest, it is this aspect of the novel's formal richness, in tandem with its imagery, which 'creates lateral understanding' (Beer, 1986, 192).

Repetition, Difference and Discrimination

To give an example, we have seen already that George Eliot makes her reader do early in the novel what Dorothea learns to do in the course of it – to see not just from one centre of interest but to inhabit imaginatively different points of view. Chapter 20, we saw in Chapter 1 of this book, switches abruptly back to Dorothea's unhappy honeymoon, repeating the sudden switch of attention now from Lydgate to Dorothea. As soon as the reader's interest is thoroughly absorbed, the narrative forces the reader to direct his or her sympathetic regard to a wholly different human situation. In this way, the author encourages within her reader the moral and imaginative flexibility of mind and feeling which – in varying degrees, as we shall see more fully in Chapter 3 – she is also forcing upon all her characters. Chapter 11, even in switching focus, begins to draw attention to the contrastive connectedness between the Dorothea-Casaubon story and the Lydgate-Rosamond story:

> Lydgate believed that he should not marry for several years: not marry until he had trodden out a good clear path for himself . . . He had seen Miss Vincy above his horizon almost as long as it had taken Mr Casaubon to become engaged and married: but this learned gentleman was possessed of a fortune . . . Lydgate was young, poor, ambitious. He had his half-century before him instead of behind him. (92–3)

That final sentence points ahead to Book Two of the novel, where pairings of 'Old and Young' (the book's title) abound. Yet the sentence is paradoxically played off against 'almost as long' in the second sentence, insisting upon a close temporal parallel between Casaubon's and Lydgate's current stories for all the opposing relation to present, past and future determined by the two men's respective ages. Indeed, this sense of the two stories running alongside one another in time is reinforced in the following two or three chapters by the fact that the narration now moves backwards in time to record developments up to and including the first meeting between Lydgate and Rosamond.

Thus from the closing stages of Book One onwards there is a strong sense of simultaneity in these narrative strands – a sense of the other story carrying on even where it is temporarily out of sight – and of ironical contrasts and comparisons, which are not heavily signposted but offered or created 'by the mere dismissal of one character or group and the reappearance of another'. The result of the related stories and of their myriad successes and failures is a novel with 'an extraordinary sense of expanding life':

> We feel the pressure of an enormous number of human beings, similar and dissimilar, modifying the doctrines of the author as well as contributing to them . . . The human examples are always variations of the theme rather than examples of it. (Hardy, 1959, 96, 93, 143).

It is this abundant multiplication and repetition – many similar things going on simultaneously at different levels of self and society and often (as Chapter 3 will illustrate) crossing the private and public realms – which makes this highly-wrought novel seem almost loose and diffuse in structure: Henry James called it a 'treasure-house of details but . . . an indifferent whole.'[16] But George Eliot's own conception of an artistic 'whole' saw it as creatively emergent from the treasure of detail. In 'Notes on Form in Art', an essay written only several years before *Middlemarch* was begun, and one that is intensely Feuerbachian,[17] she wrote that 'form as an element of human experience must begin with the perception of separateness . . . Things must be recognized as separate wholes before they can be recognized as wholes composed of parts, or before these wholes again can be regarded as relatively parts of a larger whole.' She goes on:

> Form, then . . . must first depend on the discrimination of wholes and then on the discrimination of parts . . . And as knowledge continues to grow by its alternating processes of distinction and combination, seeing smaller and smaller unlikenesses and grouping or associating these under a common likeness, it arrives at the conception of wholes composed of parts more and more multiplied and highly differenced, yet more and more absolutely bound together by various conditions of common likeness and dependence. (Ashton, 1992, 355–6)

This is a vision of a whole that depends for its authority upon a proper discrimination of parts or of separated wholes, which then yield, or out of which are discovered, a larger connected whole. The relation of this conception of form to the formal method of *Middlemarch* has long been recognized.[18] The novel holds together a multiplicity of separated worlds – Dorothea, Lydgate, Casaubon, Rosamond, Fred, Mary, Mr Bulstrode, Mrs Bulstrode – all of which are faithfully preserved not just in their social and personal individuality but in their time-bound, flesh-and-blood relative integrity. As we read these narratives forward we are continually encouraged, by virtue of their existing together, side by side, in the same novel, to think or make connections sideways.

Yet the suggestion in 'Notes on Form in Art' is that the finely accurate discernment of *difference* is what enables a more exact recognition of the 'various' relations by which the parts are bound together or connected. Eliot gave similarly explicit priority to unlikeness, multiplicity and difference in the very last work that she wrote:

> To discern likeness amidst diversity, it is well known, does not require so fine a mental edge as the discerning of diversity amidst general sameness. The primary rough classification depends upon the prominent resemblances of things: the progress is towards finer and finer discrimination according to minute differences.[19]

George Eliot seems to demonstrate retrospectively here the principles upon which her greatest novel was built. It is through the minute discrimination and tracing of the parts that we begin to find relations or connections where we had not expected to find them – between, to take examples from Chapter 3, Bulstrode and Dorothea, Lydgate and Caleb Garth, Farebrother and Will; connections which at the same time encourage recognition of the subtlety of difference that separates people one from another in terms of their drives, needs, motivations and desires. The model of multiplication, separation and recombination is closer to the cellular biology that was to supersede Lydgate's emphasis on primary tissue. A reader feels that he or she could go on and on finding connections between character and situations that bring them into ever-new forms of creative combination.

Book Six is a good example of the subtle yet absolute relationship between minute discrimination and overlap. Its title, 'The Widow and the Wife', directs us to points of similarity and contrast between Rosamond and Dorothea. From being separate worlds with distinct if analogous dreams in Book One (both look to an outsider to fulfil their lives), their lots have converged so that they are now two points on a love triangle involving Will. The key area of overlap is that of marriage. The contrast between the two women as wives is suggested most powerfully in Chapter 58, where Lydgate speaks to Rosamond of their financial difficulties, and says 'You must help me':

> 'What can *I* do, Tertius?' said Rosamond, turning her eyes on him again. That little speech of four words, like so many others in all languages, is capable by varied vocal inflexions of expressing all states of mind from helpless dimness to exhaustive argumentative perception, from the completest self-devoting fellowship to the

most neutral aloofness. Rosamond's thin utterance threw into the words: 'What can *I* do!' as much neutrality as they could hold. They fell like a mortal chill on Lydgate's roused tenderness. He did not storm in indignation – he felt too sad a sinking of the heart. And when he spoke again it was more in the tone of a man who forced himself to fulfil a task. (585)

George Eliot's mind and language is here at its most micro-surgically fine and exact, in its analysis of the plenitude of implication in Rosamond's thin utterance. No one could be more superficial, we feel at this moment, than Rosamond. But the narrator's presence here gives a sense of depth and meaning even to Rosamond's lack of deep meaning by showing what that lack itself means to Lydgate, how much he feels her lack of feeling. George Eliot's friend, the evolutionary psychologist Herbert Spencer, called 'cadence' (used 'in an unusually extended sense, as comprehending all modifications of voice') the 'commentary of the emotions upon the propositions of the intellect'.[20] The novel itself demonstrates how the question 'What can I do?' can be put into expression in an infinite variety of ways. Its variations occur and recur repeatedly in the novel across character-groupings and situations – 'What could she do, what ought she to do?', 'What shall you do?', 'What was he to do?' – as if it were a gene of helplessness susceptible to the whole range of human experiment. The same urgent questioning scattered throughout the novel and from character to character suggests, quite as much as the fully-realized setting, a community of characters 'moving . . . in the same embroiled medium, the same troublous, fitfully-illuminated life' (Hardy, 1959, 168).

Yet the novel at the same time schools us literally to remember where same is also not the same. Rosamond's tonal absence of feeling is a complete difference of meaning from 'that little speech of four words' as it is used by Dorothea to Lydgate in respect of her husband's ailing health: 'Advise me. Think what I can do. He has been labouring all his life and looking forward. He minds about nothing else. And I mind about nothing else' (287). Directly before his conversation with Rosamond, the speech has echoed in Lydgate's mind:

That voice of deep-souled womanhood had remained within him as the enkindling conceptions of dead and sceptred genius had remained within him . . . the tones were a music from which he was falling away – he had really fallen into a momentary doze, when Rosamond said in her silvery neutral way, 'Here is your tea, Tertius'. (583)

The narrative means us not only to remember the distinction but to hear it in the contrast between Dorothea's 'deep-souled voice' and Rosamond's 'silvery neutral' tone. It is in the distinction between them that Lydgate *hears* the sound of his own wasted life, in as primitive a way as Bulstrode *saw* his salvation in the death of Raffles, and in as direct and sensory a way as Dorothea recognizes that Casaubon has 'an equivalent centre of self'. For all its potentially consoling lateral connectedness, *Middlemarch* is always faithful to the integrity of the terrible individual movements from shallows to depths, and of the impossibility of these conjoined individuals to help one another with the troubles they share in common. 'But what could he say now', is Lydgate's inward response to Dorothea's plea, 'except say that he should see Mr Casaubon tomorrow' (287). This closeness to Hardyesque *fin-de-siècle* absence of consolation is an aspect of the novel to which Chapter 3 will return.

REALISM

The nineteenth century was the great age of realism, and *Middlemarch* is the supreme exemplar of the genre in the Victorian period. One reason why George Eliot's finest novel is synonymous with realism for many people ('To the impatient question, What do you *mean* by realism?, it is tempting just to lift the novel high and say, I mean THIS' (Chase, 1991)) is that she was one of the few practitioners of the mode who left some definitive statements on the realist method and why she found it conducive. One of the problems with defining the term 'realism' or 'realist' is the absence of an organized or systematic body of theory such as was produced by the Romantics, or by the late nineteenth-century naturalists, or by the surrealists of the early twentieth century. The realist writers of the nineteenth century did not come up with an artistic policy or statement of their aims. Partly this is because it is in the nature of realism to avoid the abstract and systematic and remain true to the messiness of things as they are. As 'a bundle of experiences', 'an unabating interest in the shapes and relations of the real world', an unambiguous commitment to the 'ballast, rubble, detritus [which weigh down this world]' (Stern, 55, 135, 171), realism is a mode thus resistant to category, since it is inherently amorphous. Moreover, polished theories about one's art do not seem consistent with an artistic mission to record humdrum ordinary life. Statements about literary realism's ideals and practices tend, therefore, to be dotted about in letters, in occasional essays, in prefaces to works of fiction, or even inside the novels themselves.

One of George Eliot's most famous statements on the matter comes in her first full-length novel, and the work which made her name, *Adam Bede*. In Chapter 17, the author deliberately halts the narrative flow to offer a declaration of her aims as a writer:

> I aspire to give no more than a faithful account of men and things as they have mirrored themselves in my mind. The mirror is doubtless defective; the outlines will sometimes be disturbed; the reflection faint or confused; but I feel as much bound to tell you, as precisely as I can, what that reflection is, as if I were in the witness-box narrating my experience on oath.[21]

Realism for George Eliot meant telling the truth as precisely and, as we shall see, as inclusively as possible. As a writer, her constant anxiety was that each new novel might be less '*true*' and worth less as a result.[22] Yet here she concedes that the notion of art as straightforward truth-telling has its shortcomings: 'The mirror is doubtless defective.' The truth her story offers is as necessarily determined by her particular point of view, outlook or position as individual perspective is shown to be limited, partial and relative in *Middlemarch*. Another witness in the witness box, to continue her analogy, would likely have seen the same events differently. What Eliot begins to outline here is precisely the problem that preoccupied critics of realism as a genre in the last quarter of the twentieth century. The 'truth' of the nineteenth-century novel was at best historically contingent, it was claimed: appropriate to a world that could take for granted a common sense of reality, but outmoded in an age characterized by fragmentedness and multiplicity.[23] At worst it is a confidence trick (albeit a naively perpetrated one), which passes off an ideologically derived and conservative *version* of reality for reality itself, and thus collaborates in the oppressive operation of the dominant ideology. Realism's habit of concealing its acquiescence in the ideology of the governing class – by offering itself as a transparent window on reality – makes its (hidden) endorsement of prevailing power structures all the more powerful.[24] As language is always culturally mediated, this argument goes, literary realism (as against the visual realism of pictorial art) can never be the conduit or purveyor of pure truth.

No one knew better than a writer with the linguistic and literary range of George Eliot, however, how clumsy and often crude is the relation of language to the truths it purports to represent. She goes on to say in Chapter 17 of *Adam Bede*:

> Falsehood is so easy, truth so difficult . . . Examine your words well, and you will find that even when you have no motive to be false, it's a very hard thing to say the exact truth, even about your own immediate feelings – much harder than to say something fine about them which is *not* the exact truth. (*Adam Bede*, 176–7)

George Eliot recognized as completely as T. S. Eliot, writing over half a century later, that words are slippery things which crack, strain and break under the burden of trying to make accurate meaning. The response of the modernists, however, and especially of the postmodernists of the twentieth century, was to become more and more distrustful and sceptical of the power of words to tell the truth, creating fictions which deliberately drew attention to the difficulties these writers experience with representing reality. Modernist works were often disjointed, fragmentary and unreaderly, in order that readers could not succumb to the cosy illusion that what they were witnessing as they read was real life. Where twentieth-century writers largely gave up on the realist project, the nineteenth-century writers felt that the more difficult it was to produce accurate representation in language, the harder they must try to get it right – to hit on the exact truth by staying close to the details, the particulars, the minutiae of real life as they saw it. 'The truth of infinite value that he teaches', said George Eliot of her contemporary John Ruskin,

> is *realism* – the doctrine that all truth and beauty are to be attained by a humble and faithful study of nature, and not by substituting vague forms, bred by imagination on the mists of feeling, in place of definite substantial reality. The thorough acceptance of this doctrine would remould our life. ('Review of Modern Painters III', 1856, in Ashton, 1992, 248)

The realist was committed to the minutely careful and exact observation of particulars, in place of the kind of generalizations or idealizations which belonged to earlier literary traditions. Many of our commonsense or shorthand definitions of realism are essentially derived from what George Eliot's novels do. 'Ordinary' individual lives are presented as embedded in social and material conditions that are depicted in circumstantial detail and which are shown to be continuous in complex ways with personal psychology.

Yet some important interpretations of literary realism consider it (very usefully in respect of *Middlemarch*) as a historically determined 'disposition' rather than a genre. Realism, on this reading, is a 'middle mode which has its being between two extremes' – those of absolute religious belief on the one hand, and absolute lack of belief on the other. 'Ages in which [the problem of the world's connectedness with the divine] is not at issue, either because the presence of the divine is taken for granted (as in the Middle Ages) or because its absence is (as in our own time), are not favourable to literary realism' (Stern, 171–3). The 'middle distance' of realism engenders and enables 'formal agreement about the conditions of perception'. It primarily represents 'not the "objects" supposedly contained "in" time and space, but precisely the common denominators themselves, neutral time and neutral space: and particularly the power they confer to deliver mutual relevance even between the most disparate events or persons':

> The genial consensus of realistic narration implies a unity in human experience which assures us that we all inhabit the same world and that the same meanings are available to everyone . . . However refracted it may be by point of view and by circumstance, the uniformity at the base of human experience and the solidarity of human nature receive confirmation from realistic conventions . . . Realist novels demonstrate the power of narrative consciousness to occupy one mind after another; and in so doing, they confirm the potential continuity of consciousness between minds and even implicitly extend that continuity beyond the arbitrary limits of the text to include the reader. The narrator transgresses the boundaries of individuality not only between persons but also between persons and text . . . A stable invariant world is there . . . *because* everybody agrees that it is so. (Ermarth, 1983, xix–xx, 50, 65–7, 77)

An agnostic age produced, in the formal conventions of the realist novel, the means to believe in the wholeness of the created world: 'The most complex total reality which [humanity] could once imagine was God. Realism is the attempt to grasp that totality in terms of [humanity]: [humanity] with its "stolen essence" – as Feuerbach defined God – restored to [it].'[25]

Structuralist and deconstructionist readings unpicked and exposed the conventional basis of realism's project of totalizing consensus, as we shall see in Chapter 5. More recent sympathetic readings have recognized the degree to which *Middlemarch* effectively deconstructs itself and offers the kind of rich indeterminacy and openness prized by current literary-theoretical and critical trends.[26] But the novel's abundance of meanings is not simply a matter of 'play', since its revelations are often more austere and troubling than they are gratuitously gleeful. A realist novel like *Middlemarch* is uniquely placed, says Raymond Tallis, to demonstrate how the great 'unspoken, implicit or suppressed distances' are *within* the real world, and not between the real and the fictional one. With the realist novelist's imaginative effort to enter the interiority of other selves comes the disclosure that 'the actual world is not a unity and there are many worlds within "the world" ':

> The most fundamentally decentring and estranging intuition is that we do not see ourselves as others see us or see or experience the world as others experience it. Writing realist fiction, imagining the actual, is a way of honouring that redeeming intuition. (Tallis, 15, 207–8)

The nineteenth-century realist novel, *Middlemarch* above all, came into being at the inception of the relativistic world which is the modern inheritance as part of a culture's strenuous effort to make terms with and, if possible, redeem that relativism. The 'struggling, erring human creatures' whom George Eliot depicts in the characters of *Middlemarch* as they try to come to terms with their own mistakes, failures, defeats and frustrations are offered as particularized and moving representations of the Dorotheas, Lydgates and Casaubons who exist outside the novel. If the reader can be made to imagine and feel with the literally unshareable loneliness of the characters in the realist novel then, the hope (often dimly) is, fellow-feeling and sympathy can be extended to the real creatures in real life for whom these characters stand. 'Art is the nearest thing to life; it is a mode of amplifying experience and extending our contact with our fellow-men beyond the bounds of our personal lot' ('The Natural History of German Life', in Ashton, 1992, 263–4).

For all its agnosticism, *Middlemarch* represents a form of belief. Thus recent attempts to rehabilitate George Eliot as a precursor of modernist scepticism – *Middlemarch*'s ideological opposite – largely miss the point of her realism. Her writings about realism as much as her practice in the form show that, as Isobel Armstrong has put it, 'the nature of the experiencing subject, the problems of representation, fiction and language, are just as much the heart of Victorian problems as they are the preoccupations of modernism. The difference is that the Victorians see them as problems, the modernists do not.'[27]

NOTES

1 W. C. Brownell (1901) in Haight, 171, 178.
2 See Chapter 4, p. 102 below.
3 David Lodge, '*Middlemarch* and the Idea of the Classic Realist Text' in Peck (1992), 54–5.
4 Derek Oldfield, 'The Language of the Novel: The Character of Dorothea' in Hardy (1967), 81.
5 Elizabeth Deeds Ermarth, 'Negotiating *Middlemarch*' in Chase (2006), 111–12.
6 See George Steiner (1954), 'A Preface to *Middlemarch*' in *Nineteenth-Century Fiction*, 9, 262–9.
7 See, for example, 'The Art of Fiction' (1884) in Gard (1987), 194–7.
8 Colin MacCabe, 'The End of a Metalanguage: From George Eliot to *Dubliners*' (1978) in Newton (1991), 159.
9 See Oldfield in Hardy (1967), 83 and Pascal, 79.
10 The analogy has become a critical commonplace but for a new spin; see Michael Davis (2006), 1–9.
11 See Witmeyer, 41–3 and McSweeney, 105 for more detailed discussion of this scene.
12 See Jerome Beaty (1961), *Middlemarch from Notebook to Novel: A Study in George Eliot's Creative Method*. Urbana: University of Illinois Press.
13 See Gerard Genette, trans. Jane E. Lewin (1980), *Narrative Discourse*. Oxford: Basil Blackwell, 33–5. Distinguishes 'story' and 'narrative'.
14 Quentin Anderson (1958), 'George Eliot in *Middlemarch*' in Haight, 277.
15 Interpretations of web imagery have made it contested ground, and I will reserve full study until Chapter 5.

16 '*Middlemarch*' (1873) in Gard (1987), 75.

17 See Byatt (1990), xxxi.

18 See, for example, Beer (1996), Byatt (1990), Chase (1991), Carroll (1992).

19 D. J. Enright (ed.) (1995), George Eliot (1879), *The Impressions of Theophrastus Such*. London: Everyman, 135.

20 'The Origin and Function of Music' (1883) in *Essays Scientific, Political and Speculative*. London: Williams and Norgate, I, 232.

21 Valentine Cunningham (ed.) (1996) *Adam Bede*. Oxford: Oxford University Press, 175.

22 See, for example Cross, ii, 74; Redinger, 385.

23 'We are saddled with all kinds of relativistic structures of consciousness. We do not believe in there being "one reality" as Tolstoy undoubtedly did.' Berbard Bergonzi, quoted in Damien Grant (1970), *Realism*. London: Methuen, 4.

24 See especially Catherine Belsey (1980), *Critical Practice*. London. Methuen.

25 John Berger (1969), *Art and Revolution*. London: Weidenfeld and Nicholson Ltd, 52.

26 See Chase (2006), 9; Wright, 38.

27 Isobel Armstrong (1993), *Victorian Poetry: Poetry, Poetics and Politics*. London: Routledge, 7.

STUDY QUESTIONS

1 It has been suggested that the most interesting character in *Middlemarch* is that of the narrator. Consider the function, tone, quality and 'personality' of the narrative voice in the passages cited for detailed analysis in Chapter 3.

2 Chapter 3 will begin to look at how a further image cluster relating (loosely) to windows/mirrors/reflections/water begins to emerge or accumulate across narrative strands. Consider this image pattern in the light of the propositions (more usually offered in relation to the dominant image of the web, and detailed in Chapter 4 below) that the novel's imagery provides its (a) unity (Harvey); (b) openness (Beer); (c) ideological incoherence (Eagleton and Miller).

3 '*Middlemarch* is not held together by some overarching moral perspective; it is held together by *our* learning to perform many and diverse acts of sympathy' (Chase, 1991). Do you agree that the unity of this novel has to be receptively and responsively earned by the reader?

CHAPTER 3

READING *MIDDLEMARCH*

'George Eliot's intentions are extremely complex,' says a Henry James character. 'The mass is for each detail and each detail is for the mass.' The sentence brilliantly summarizes at once the density of implication contained even in the tiniest particularity of a novel like *Middlemarch*, and the subtle inter-relatedness of those particularities. The smallest detail is packed with potential connectedness to apparently distinct episodes, concerns, situations and characters elsewhere in the novel. Of course, this dynamic is related to the pattern of ironic parallels and illuminating reflections discussed in Chapter 2: but that very pattern determines how we read each element of it. As we read closely and deeply, we must *think* widely too. George Eliot was the great literary thinker of her generation and she meant her reader to think with her. This chapter will focus on close reading of particular passages while demonstrating how they contribute to or encourage more generalized understanding.

EVOLUTION AND REVOLUTION

George Eliot wrote that in *Middlemarch* she wanted the novel to show the 'gradual action of ordinary causes' (*Letters*, V, 168). Yet, as the last chapter has already illustrated, this novel is equally committed to 'epochs' (208) in experience: the moments of decisive change. Chapter 28, in which Dorothea and her husband have returned from honeymoon to their marital home at Lowick, is a good example of how these movements simultaneously diverge and converge in this novel. Looking out from her blue-green boudoir 'the distant flat shrank in uniform whiteness and low-hanging uniformity of cloud'; inside the room 'the very furniture . . . seemed to have shrunk since she saw it before' (270–1). In this deathly environment, Dorothea stands emphatically for life, but a life attenuated and disillusioned. 'Her blooming full-pulsed youth stood there in a moral imprisonment which made itself one with the chill colourless narrowed landscape'; 'The duties of her married life, contemplated as so great beforehand, seemed to be shrinking with the furniture' (271–2). It is Dorothea's 'crisis of disenchantment . . . the dispelling of a dream', and one instance among multiple examples in this novel where George Eliot's moral version of the Copernican revolution forces characters 'from the centre to the periphery, from the dream of self which filled the world to a reduced consciousness'. In Dorothea's story, 'the disenchanted day-lit room' is 'the physical enclosure, the daily life, the woman's place . . . The forcible reduction is in part at least the realisation of the woman's lot, and the image of the room is the appropriate feminine image of the shut-in life'.[1]

Dorothea's blue-green boudoir and the view from its bow-window recur significantly at almost all key episodes of Dorothea's process of disillusion and inner growth.[2] Dorothea's own habitual projection of her inner life onto the outer world of Lowick, as she repeatedly measures the changes which have taken place in her life against the evolution of her relationship to the objects within and surrounding the blue-grey room, makes the room a compellingly and claustrophobically immediate objectification of her inward change. Yet the room becomes 'inwoven' (322) with Dorothea's intense inner life in ways less available to Dorothea's own consciousness, when her 'wandering gaze' lights upon the miniature of Mr Casaubon's aunt Julia, she 'who had made the unfortunate marriage – Will Ladislaw's grandmother':

> Dorothea could fancy that it was alive now – the delicate woman's face which yet had a headstrong look, a peculiarity difficult to interpret. Was it only her friends who thought her marriage unfortunate? or did she herself find it out to be a mistake, and taste the salt bitterness of her tears in the merciful silence of the night? What breadths of experience Dorothea seemed to have passed over since she first looked at this miniature! She felt a new companionship with it, as if it had an ear for her and could see how she was looking at it. Here was a woman who had known some difficulty about marriage. Nay, the colours deepened, the

lips and chin seemed to get larger, the hair and eyes seemed to be sending out light, the face was masculine and beamed on her with that full gaze which tells her on whom it falls that she is too interesting for the slightest movement of her eyelid to pass unnoticed and uninterpreted. The vivid presentation came like a pleasant glow to Dorothea: she felt herself smiling, and turning from the miniature sat down and looked up as if she were again talking to a figure in front of her. (272–3)

The moment is powerfully suggestive of Dorothea's own 'glowing', 'healthful', 'warm' life. Dorothea's vital life-energy here vividly 'brings to life', transformingly, the image before her, an energy which then in its turn transforms her – 'she felt herself smiling'. 'The desiring gaze with which the image of Ladislaw looks at her is simply a reflection of her own wish to be desired by him', says one critic (Wright, 48). Yet it is the reductive 'simply' of that sentence which George Eliot's realist prose typically opposes. There is no question that the 'desiring gaze' is expressive reflectively of Dorothea's own intense emotional need and perhaps unconscious sexual desire for Will, feelings which in this psychic interlude catch her out pre-consciously. The return to self-consciousness comes with the immediately succeeding recollection of Will's 'cruel' words in Rome about the futility of her husband's research, and the responsive smile at the miniature is now guiltily atoned for in 'the irresistible impulse to go and see her husband and inquire if she could do anything for him' (273).

Yet, as in the episode which, significantly, Dorothea here recalls, emergent and unacknowledged desire manifests itself in a complex of guilt, fear and alarm. 'I wanted to ask you again', she tells Will in Chapter 22, 'about something you said the other day':

'I have been thinking about it; and it seems to me that with Mr Casaubon's learning he must have before him the same materials as German scholars has he not?' Dorothea's timidity was due to an indistinct consciousness that she was in the strange situation of consulting a third person about the adequacy of Mr Casaubon's learning. (218)

In her very effort – loyally, for his sake – to rehabilitate her husband's scholarly reputation in this younger relative's eyes, she finds herself involuntarily starting to separate from Casaubon, now alienatedly strung between two opposing worldviews, instead of identified with that of the man to whose life she has united her own:

> 'How can you bear to speak so lightly?' said Dorothea, with a look between sorrow and anger. 'If it were as you say, what could be sadder than so much ardent labour all in vain?' . . . She was beginning to be shocked that she had got to such a point of supposition, and indignant with Will for having led her to it. (219)

The life-energy of *Middlemarch*, as we saw in Chapter 1, is often generated not by events themselves but by these tiny, unsignalled 'beginnings', the 'indistinct', in-between 'lurking-places' where desire or change originates or starts to know itself.[3] The vision of process which informs the novel as a whole emphasizes not visible nor dramatic change but the hidden, subtle, slow, 'drip, drip, drip' effect of accumulated experience:

> That new real future which was replacing the imaginary drew its material from the endless minutiae by which her view of Mr Casaubon and her wifely relation, now that she was married to him, was gradually changing with the secret motion of a watch-hand from what it had been in her maiden dream. (192)

George Eliot's gradualism is an intense teasing out of the subtly emergent and 'secret' transitions by which change turns out, in the novel's moments of catch-up, to have become an embedded and acknowledged part of her life. 'Sorrow comes in so many ways,' Dorothea says to Will in Chapter 54:

> 'Two years ago I had no notion of that – I mean of the unexpected way in which trouble comes, and ties our hands, and makes us silent when we long to speak. I used to despise women a little for not shaping their lives more, and doing better things. I was very fond of doing as I liked, but I have almost given it up,' she ended smiling playfully. (537)

We do not see the moment when Dorothea (ruefully) lets go of her dream of an ideally-shaped life (that 'almost' indicates that no such absolute sacrifice has anyway taken place and perhaps never could for a Dorothea). The near-abandonment has been the cumulative and dispersed result of those successive tests and mistakes through which her life has – for the most part hiddenly and implicitly – shaped her.

But this novel is equally interested, by contrast, in how primary experience of change, as a visible, or temporally-appointed life event, becomes part of the suffering transformation. Take, for instance, the moment when Dorothea learns of the codicil to Casaubon's will:

> She might have compared her experience at that moment to the vague, alarmed consciousness that her life was taking on a new form, that she was undergoing a metamorphosis in which memory would not adjust itself to the stirring of new organs. Everything was changing its aspect: her husband's conduct, her own duteous feeling towards him, every struggle between them – and yet more, her whole relation to Will Ladislaw. Her world was in a state of convulsive change; the only thing she could say distinctly to herself was, that she must wait and think anew. (483)

Change for Dorothea here is not a matter of casting off her old self and emerging into a new. Rather her old self and past life is suddenly and shockingly re-cast and reconfigured by the events of the present, while still – confusingly and incoherently – co-existing in the present, unaltered, as 'memory' that 'would not adjust itself'. The biological image is striking here.[4] A moment of profound incoherence is experienced, the image insists, deep down into physical being. Yet even amid this change, and perhaps because of it, there is another process at work here – a coming into awareness or explicitness of what already exists or has already been formed in character:

> Then again she was conscious of another change which also made her tremulous; it was a sudden strange yearning of heart towards Will Ladislaw. It had never before entered her mind that he could, under any circumstances, be her lover: conceive the effect of the sudden revelation that another had thought of him in that light – that perhaps he himself had been conscious of such a possibility. (483)

The emergent recognition of her love for Will is the beginning of Dorothea's acceptance of her own sexual needs. When she experiences that 'sudden strange yearning of heart' she is not so much changing as finding herself. Yet that moment of self-discovery is deeply involuntary, forced upon her from the outside by 'the sudden revelation that *another* had thought of him as her lover'. George Eliot is not implicitly criticizing Dorothea's resistance to self-recognition here: it is the repeated insight of this novel that what a person really is, may be what he or she is least able to see for himself or herself (think of Casaubon, Farebrother and Bulstrode). Rather the novel is demonstrating the complexity of the process by which character is formed and reformed, made and found, with and against the individual's settled idea of self.

Yet this does not complete the process begun in those earlier scenes. For the 'full gaze' which Dorothea sees imaged in the miniature is itself only one aspect (albeit the most intense and affecting one) of her desire for a 'sense of connexion with a manifold pregnant existence', which connection 'had to be kept up painfully as an inward vision, instead of coming from without in claims that would have shaped her energies' (272). The very first call to life that Dorothea experiences amid the deadening disenchantment of her gentlewoman's room comes from sympathetic identification with another woman (Mr Casaubon's aunt Julia) who has made an 'unfortunate marriage'. The sensitive ability to 'have an ear for' another, to 'see' with another person's troubled vision, which Dorothea attributes to the miniature, is actually a projection of Dorothea's own humane capacities. In the 'new companionship' that Dorothea feels with the miniature of aunt Julia, it is as if Dorothea's painfully kept-up 'inward vision' finds momentary translation into a form of outward, outgoing energy. Yet it is shaped not only by a sudden sense of claims from without but by the 'breadths of experience' Dorothea has traversed within. It is the unhappy experience of her own mistake that enables her to respond with sympathetic, sentient comprehension to the similar mistakes of another, just as the painful awareness of her own sorrow led her to appreciate an 'equivalent' sorrow in Casaubon. The extraordinary resonance of this moment in the novel comes from its not being 'simply' a symptom of repressed sexuality, or of the narrowly egoistic tendencies Dorothea displayed when she saw 'reflected' in Mr Casaubon's mind 'every quality she herself brought' (23), although both are part of the impure mix of the moment's power. These passages in Dorothea's growth towards sexual maturity and self-knowledge are complexly and confusingly (for Dorothea) related to her moral growth, and are as past-dependent as they are future-oriented. George Eliot's gradualist, inclusive mode makes even the most decisive moment of the novel inisolable. The real completion of this sequence occurs in the famous scene in Chapter 80 in which Dorothea sees from her window a landscape which, though the same, is startlingly unfamiliar for being recognized as existing, separatedly, outside of her. It marks her emergence from self-absorbed perception to one which, in every sense, looks out.

SELF AND WORLD

> Some gentlemen have made an amazing figure in literature by general discontent with the universe as a trap for dulness into which their great souls have fallen by mistake; but the sense of a stupendous self and an insignificant world may have its consolations . . . [Lydgate's] troubles will perhaps appear miserably sordid, and beneath the attention of lofty persons who can know nothing of debt except on a magnificent scale. Doubtless they were sordid; and for the majority, who are not lofty, there is no escape from sordidness but by being free from money-craving. (637)

In the story of Lydgate and in the analogous situations of other major characters, the novel is (avowedly here) going beyond the conventional Romantic preoccupation with the opposition between self and world to a concern with the world and society as the necessary condition and means by which an individual makes his or her way.[5] ('Money-craving', as we shall see later in this chapter, no one in Middlemarch can afford – literally in many cases – to consider 'sordid'.) Critics have long been divided over George Eliot's sense of the relation between individual and society. For some twentieth-century critics, what underpinned and generated the failures depicted in *Middlemarch* was the author's essentially deterministic world-view – the belief that society, and the universe generally, runs along mechanistic lines in the face of which the human individual, however aspiring, is finally impotent.[6] Counter-responses to these criticisms sought to stress the degree of character responsibility.[7] The evidence of the novel is that to try to weigh the relative importance of individual and society is to miss the point of George Eliot's focus. Self and world both do, and do not, have separate existences or influences in passages like the following, from Chapter 58 and Chapter 64 respectively:

> Lydgate was aware that his concessions to Rosamond were often little more than the lapse of slackening resolution, the creeping paralysis apt to seize an enthusiasm which is out of adjustment to a constant portion of our lives. And on Lydgate's enthusiasm there was constantly pressing not a simple weight of sorrow, but the biting presence of a petty degrading care, such as casts the blight of irony over all higher effort . . . Lydgate was in debt; and he could not succeed in keeping out of his mind for long together that he was every day getting deeper into that swamp, which tempts men towards it with such a pretty covering of flowers and verdure. It is wonderful how soon a man gets up to his chin there – in a condition in which, spite of himself, he is forced to think chiefly of release, though he had a scheme of the universe in his soul. (577–8)

> The pressure of sordid cares [had so tightened] on Lydgate's mind that is was hardly possible for him to think unbrokenly of any other subject, even the most habitual and soliciting. He was not an ill-tempered man; his intellectual activity, the ardent kindness of his heart, as well as his strong frame, would always, under tolerably easy conditions, have kept him above the petty uncontrolled susceptibilities which make bad temper. But he was now a prey to that worst irritation which arises not simply from annoyance, but from the second consciousness underlying those annoyances, of wasted energy, and a degrading preoccupation, which was the reverse of all his former purposes. '*This* is what I am thinking of; and *that* is what I might have been thinking of', was the bitter incessant murmur within him, making every difficulty a double goad to impatience. (637)

These passages seem to witness social forces, or what is outside of self, turning, almost visibly, into what is inside – into character and being – in a complex process of transmission. The 'slackening resolution' which produces Lydgate's concessions to Rosamond in the first passage, for instance, is not only the knock-on effect of Lydgate's sense that he is getting deeper into a worsening situation that there is no point in any longer trying to control. What also

creates that 'creeping paralysis' is Lydgate's sense of the lack of correspondence between his inward and outward life – his appalled
recognition of the massive disproportion, in terms both of size and
power, between the grandeur of his ambitions and the pettiness of
the external frustrations. For the smallness without – 'the biting
presence of a petty degrading care', the desperate necessity to release
himself from debt – is not only incommensurate with, but threaten-
ing to overwhelm the largeness within, the 'higher effort', the soul's
'scheme of the universe'. It is this lack of 'adjustment' *between* the
inner and outer life – and not simply the influence of one or the other
– that is producing Lydgate's bitter sense of 'irony' and thus turning
into who he is. In the second passage the process has gone further or
deeper. Neither his even temper, his elasticity of disposition, nor his
physical strength, not even his good mind and good heart, nothing
of what is best in him, can help Lydgate to resist, transcend or break
the absorption of his energy in the petty irritations pressing upon
him from without. Yet that very absorption is made all the more
intolerable by the fact that the whole man is *not* consumed by
thought of debt. For the annoyances of his situation have produced
– as though it were a new growth, aspect or dimension of self – a
'second consciousness underlying those annoyances', which looks
on at the misery and waste of his life, 'incessantly' and tormentedly
registering the distance between what is and 'what might have been',
yet doing so helplessly and with a bitter sense of its own redundancy.
It is as if failure helps to produce in Lydgate the capacity to take full
measure of his failure, and that capacity in turn puts him the more
psychologically in failure's thrall.

Writing of the way in which George Eliot 'exhibits her characters
to us in the making,' James Sully (a contemporary psychologist and
friend of George Eliot) said:

> I have observed that the distinction between the characters and
> plot of a novel is only a rough distinction. This remark applies
> with special force to George Eliot's stories. These appear in a
> remarkable degree, when regarded from one point of view as the
> outcome of her characters, from another point of view as the for-
> mation of these characters.[8]

Sully's remarks help to show that the point is not whether Lydgate
should have been better (though he might have been) or that society

should have been more accommodating (though it could have been). The point is that the novel is holding together, in solution as it were, all of the forces – heredity, education, social class, historical location, professions and so on – which the author sees as constantly acting and reacting upon one another. Lydgate's story is both the formation *and* the outcome of his character, as his life shapes itself (tragically enough) through the interplay of his self and his situation. The reciprocal action of character and circumstance is delicately and scrupulously tense. The 'balance of forces'[9] is explicitly evident in the novel's pronouncements on the relation of individual to circumstance, not only within them, syntactically – 'It always remains true that if we had been greater, circumstance would have been less strong against us' (577) – but across or between them, perspectively. Looked at one way, it is the individual who is to blame; looked at another, it is 'circumstance'. Hence: 'There is no creature whose inward being is so strong that it is not greatly determined by what lies outside it' (821). The emphasis shifts, not mechanically or arbitrarily, but because it is in the nature of the rich interchange between self and world in this novel that the exact terms of that relation should be in constant dynamic flux. For 'character too is a process and an unfolding': both an outcome and a revelation, not one or the other, or one after the other, but both together, fluidly and unpredictably.

The dynamism persists from the beginning to end of Lydgate's story. For as the stress at the outset of his story is upon possibility or potential, the man 'in the making' – 'he was at a starting-point which makes many a man's career a fine subject for betting . . . there were both virtues and faults capable of shrinking or expanding' (147) – so in the very last episode in which we see him with Dorothea, there is a strong sense, even amid the waste of his marriage and career, of a 'might have been', a second chance. In Chapter 76, Dorothea offers Lydgate the necessary money and support to allow him to continue his work in Middlemarch, and also to intercede with Rosamond on his behalf: 'Lydgate did not answer, and she saw that he was debating with himself . . . Lydgate still waited, but at last turned to speak in his most decisive tones' (755). In these hesitations there is a fleeting but strong sense of an alternative destiny for Lydgate. What prevents it seems in part to be the failing of pride, which got him into debt in the first place and thus in hock to Bulstrode; it resists 'the degradation of being pensioned for work . . .

never achieved', and recoils from being seen to have come down in the world by his neighbours: 'it is easier to make necessary changes in a new place' (756). Still, the scene never minimizes the weight of circumstance that presses upon Lydgate at this juncture: his concern for his reputation, for his wife's happiness, for his own 'creeping paralysis' and for his very capacity, therefore, to keep going – 'I have lost all spirit about carrying on my life here' (754). None of these is presented as a negligible consideration. On the contrary it is in this chapter, more than anywhere else perhaps, that we feel Lydgate's struggles against the 'petty medium' of ordinary provincial society taking on an elevatedly tragic dimension, in so far as the sense of wasted promise is acute: ' "I must do as other men do . . . that is the sort of shell I must creep into and try to keep my soul alive in' (756). Still, there is the possibility, albeit frail, that if Lydgate *had* been greater, the outcome might have been different. This moment contributes to the large margin of untried possibilities – 'that imagined "otherwise" ', as the narrator calls it in relation to Will Ladislaw (462) – which is sometimes as palpable as the fulfilled destinies.[10]

SEARCH FOR A KEY

Lydgate is nonetheless typical of this novel insofar as its characters' ideals seem to be relentlessly defeated. Casaubon's search for his 'Key to all Mythologies' defines a central theme of *Middlemarch*: the search for unity amidst plurality. Casaubon is attempting to reconcile the apparently conflicting systems of myth and lore of many different peoples and across many ages by identifying their common source. What lies behind his research is a belief in the common origins of world civilizations: the multiplicity and diversity of custom and legend are corruptions, so his theory goes, of an original, single tradition or truth. There are a number of analogous or related examples of this search in the novel, which variously compare or contrast with and comment upon one another. Casaubon's ambition is paralleled most closely by Lydgate's search for a unitary source in his anatomical investigations: 'What was the primitive tissue?', 'the common basis' (146–7) of all anatomical structures adapted to special bodily functions, the key that will explain the workings of the human organism. This search for the very origins of life is a bold biological version of Dorothea's own desire for a principle of unity to make sense of her own life, the larger life around it and the relation between the two: the 'provinces of masculine knowledge' that Mr Casaubon represents to her seem 'a standing-ground from which all truth could be seen more truly' (62); 'her usual eagerness' is 'for a binding theory which could bring her own life and doctrine into strict connexion with that amazing past, and give the remotest sources of knowledge some bearing on her actions' (84). All of these examples in turn recall Will Ladislaw's habit of seeing hidden, original wholes from visible fragments: 'He confessed that Rome had given him quite a new sense of history as a whole; the fragments stimulated his imagination and made him constructive' (209).

The pervasive effort in *Middlemarch* to penetrate or to see beyond a multiplicity of meanings or systems to some single authority that generates and explains them reflects a general trend in Victorian intellectual life – a Darwinian preoccupation with tracing, observing or creating links between the past and the present. 'In the Victorian period,' comments Gillian Beer, in her study of the relationship between the novel and evolutionary theory, 'the Romantic search for the "One Life" had been set back in time and become the search for Origins' (1983, 154). Yet the search for a key in *Middlemarch* is a symptom of the absence of 'coherent social faith and order', which, the Prelude announces, is the surrounding context and condition of the lives and events depicted in the novel. The search for unity is part of the individual compulsion – variously and repeatedly demonstrated in the novel – to create a coherent and comprehensive world-view, or 'cosmology',[11] in the absence of a divinely or socially given one. This desire to make sense of oneself and one's place in a fallen world connects the (fallacious?) coherence of Casaubon's mythological and Lydgate's anatomical systems to, for instance, Bulstrode's deviously self-serving divine scheme on the one hand ('In his closest meditations the life-long habit of Mr Bulstrode's mind clad his most egoistic terrors in doctrinal references to superhuman ends' 518), and to Mrs Cadwallader's innocently comic (and outmoded) aristocratic scheme on the other ('She believed as unquestioningly in birth and no-birth as she did in game and vermin' 58).

Critical debate as to how far the novel endorses the commitment to discovering fundamentals usually centres upon the intellectual fortunes of Casaubon and Lydgate. Casaubon's researches are, of course, exposed as futile in the course of the novel. As Will was all too glad to explain to Dorothea in Rome, Casaubon's research has already been rendered worthless by the work of German scholars in the field, and there is little reason to doubt Will's insistence that Casaubon's studies are obsolete.[12] Equally there is strong evidence to suggest that George Eliot thought of Lydgate as working at a moment in history that directly preceded the great progress made by biologists in cellular theory in the 1830s: 'The next step was to be from the tissue to the cell, and, at least from George Eliot's vantage point in 1870, the truth of biology had to do with irreducible multiplicity rather than with a unitary source.' Developments in biology, as in mythography, were both to prove, it seems, that 'there was no chance of resolving the Many into One'.[13] As we saw in the previous chapter, this is the implicit lesson of the structure of the novel, as it is the teaching of the narrator's many scientific analogies. For example:

> Even with a microscope directed on a water-drop we find ourselves making interpretations which turn out to be rather coarse; for whereas under a weak lens you may seem to see a creature exhibiting an active voracity into which other smaller creatures actively play as if they were so many animated tax-pennies, a stronger lens reveals to you certain tiniest hairlets which make vortices for these victims . . . showing a play of minute causes. (58)

The emphasis here is on the difficulty of applying general or 'coarse' explanations to phenomena, the causes of which are 'tiny', 'minute', multiple and all but impossible to distinguish one from another. As we saw at the outset of this chapter, this minutiae of causation is the tissue of the novel as much as its defining 'mental passages'.[14]

The 'cause' of Lydgate's failures as a pioneer, therefore, seems as much an irony of timing and a matter of bad luck as his mistake in marrying Rosamond. And even that colossal error of judgement, at the decisive moment when they become engaged, involves, when viewed microscopically, his strengths as much as his weaknesses, as we almost see them changing places: 'At this moment she was as natural as she had ever been when she was five years old . . . That moment of naturalness was the crystallising feather-touch: it shook flirtation into love' (298). A whole life here turns on a feather touch: elusive, delicate, fine and momentary, its effects are permanent and damaging.[15] The great irony of the scene (and of the remainder of Lydgate's unhappy life) is that Lydgate should fall for Rosamond's 'naturalness' – an aberration of the moment in a person who, except on one further occasion, is studiously, even intrinsically ('she was by nature an actress of parts' (115)) devoted to the artificial. The irony is dramatic not sceptical, however, not just because the naturalness *is* natural, involuntarily produced by the play of 'minute causes' that has unexpectedly and accidentally placed the couple together in a situation of embarrassingly charged physical proximity: the moment is crystallizing and definitive because it calls into play the aspects of Lydgate that most deeply define him, both as a man ('the ambitious man . . . was very warm-hearted and rash' (298)) and as a doctor ('he was used to being gentle with the weak and suffering' (ibid.)). Not one key or cause, but numerous influences – relating to the past as well as the present, to personal and professional character, to the novel and the known – determine this moment. 'In all failures,' the narrator says at the opening of this scene, 'the beginning is certainly the half of the whole' (297). But what this passage as a whole suggests is that there is no getting back to a 'beginning' or originating cause – a difficulty which is only compounded in view of the fact that Lydgate feels already compromised in this situation by the subtle influence of Middlemarch gossip concerning the supposed understanding between Lydgate and Rosamond: 'Momentary speculations as to the possible grounds for Mrs Bulstrode's hints had managed to get woven like slight clinging hairs into the more substantial web of his thoughts' (ibid.). Middlemarch provincial conventionalism is all the more hiddenly pervasive in its effects upon Lydgate for seeming to him so petty and insignificant. Lydgate's situation is an image of the collision and convergence of the many and the various which, in this novel, makes 'things severally go on' (290).

This apparent disjuncture between the evidence of the novel's procedure and the intellectual and emotional commitment of its characters (including, arguably, the character of the narrator[16]) has also divided critical interpretation.[17] Yet David Carroll has argued that one of the reasons for this critical polarization is that the novel characteristically gives weight to both sides of the question as to the possibility of unitary theory of life. Examples of the search for unity, and of the failures and dangers of such a totalizing quest, are both given 'urgent and plausible representation', not only through the histories of the characters but in the reading process itself. For while the novel makes us share in the individual's need for the binding theory that will resolve plurality into singleness, and difference into similarity, it continually confronts us at the same time, by its sheer range of human type and character, with 'various and subtly inconsistent theories of life':

> 'The time was gone by,' Dorothea Brooke acknowledges, 'for guiding visions and spiritual directors'. In their absence the reader experiences at first hand the life of the novel as a hypothesis continually collapsing under the weight of new evidence which the different segments of the narrative bring to light. (Carroll, 1992, 234–5)

The result is a fine balance between 'credulity and scepticism' (ibid.). Here is a version of what Elizabeth Deeds Ermarth has called that 'inevitable "on the other hand" ' in *Middlemarch*: 'All but the most carefully formulated conclusions about George Eliot seem reversible. No sooner do you say something definitive about her novels than you confront a counterbalancing consideration, a qualifying remark' (Chase, 2006, 112). This novel might well be sceptical about systems, but it explicitly recognizes that ordinary human life could not for a moment carry on without the kind of belief which accepts them: 'Scepticism, as we know, can never be thoroughly applied, else life would come to a standstill: something we must believe in and do' (238). Thus, one comes away from reading *Middlemarch* with the feeling that only the novel itself can adequately grasp and contain the multitude of readings it has generated.

VOCATION

Dorothea's repeated question – 'What could she do, what ought she to do?' (27) – articulates a critical human question for an increasingly secularized era. In an earlier age, as the Prelude suggests, a Dorothea might have found fulfilment of her 'desire to make her life greatly effective' (ibid.) in a religious calling. In the post-religious era of the mid- to late Victorian period, however, the kind of need which Dorothea expresses was almost bound to seek fulfilment in the secular activity of work. There is hardly a character in the novel (major or minor) who does not speak for, confront or represent the question of what to do with an individual life as a serious human issue.

Fred and Will

Fred Vincy has no epic ambition but his situation resonates with Dorothea's, as from major to minor key: 'What secular avocation on earth was there for a young man (whose friends could not get him an "appointment") which was at once gentlemanly, lucrative, and to be followed without special knowledge' (548). As the son of a Middlemarch manufacturer, Fred is 'inevitable heir to nothing in particular' (117). With the loss of 'coherent social faith' announced by the Prelude, traditionally settled hierarchies of rank and status were disappearing, or being replaced in a newly industrialized world. As Fred's future prospects rely upon the incalculable generosity of Featherstone's caprice in the matter of his will, so Will Ladislaw is dependent upon the income provided by his relative, Casaubon. Fred and Will thus represent a whole generation of young men in the early nineteenth century for whom the choice of career had become an issue because there was no inherited social position to bestow the gift of vocation.

In this respect *Middlemarch* is, as Henry James called it, a mode of 'history' indeed.[18] Both Fred's disappointment over the Featherstone fortune and Will's rejection of first Casaubon's, then Bulstrode's offer of patronage, is an indirect reflection of the historical-economic reality that no one in Middlemarch can evade. In this newly-commercialized English world – increasingly dominated by the middle classes and by market forces – money (literally 'a living') is something to be made or earned rather than to be passed down from one generation to the next. No one can simply opt out of such a world, for commercialism has become the condition in which the individual must survive, and which crudely levels and 'modernizes' the histori-cally older virtues embodied in heroic Lydgate, modest Farebrother and the pastoral Garths. Bulstrode's literal financial power over the people of the town is an image of the insidious, pervasive and ineluctable power of money itself in a newly mercantile capitalist age.

At another level, the paralleled situations of Will and Fred offer a paradigm of the anxiety of choice and freedom experienced in a post-traditional society. Like Fred, Will eschews the 'inconvenience' of serious application to any one pursuit or specialism in the belief that 'the intentions of the universe' will allow him to short-cut the kind of 'plodding' perseverance to which Casaubon has committed his life. Compare Fred's own 'generous reliance' upon 'the favour of provi-dence' (82, 339). But while Fred's answer is to try as far as possible to do 'nothing', Will's answer by contrast is to try to do everything – everything that is available at any rate to the embryonic 'genius' (81). Given the security of Casaubon's patronage he dabbles promiscuously in the entire range of romantic forms of expression and experience, experimenting with alcohol, asceticism and opium before passing on to a quixotic flirtation with the arts and trying out drawing, poetry, painting and sculpture in turn. Ladislaw's character is often regarded as idealized,[19] but the novel as a whole arguably goes further in exposing the dangers of Will's dilettantism than the hazards of Fred's initial indolence. The novel continually holds up the comic yet instructively negative example of Mr Brooke who 'like[s] to go into everything' (383) and achieves nothing whatever, and offers a caricature of what Will himself might become in the continued dispersal of his energies in place of settled commitment to singular pursuit. (Mr Brooke repeatedly sees in Ladislaw a younger version of himself: 255, 282.)

It is Dorothea, however, out of her own experience of a sense of 'indefiniteness' in relation to the possible uses and shape of her life, and before she has met Ladislaw, who warns against both premature decisions in respect of vocation and harsh judgments of those who may appear to be evading such decisions: 'After all, people may really have in them some vocation which is not quite plain to themselves, may they not? They may seem idle and weak because they are growing. We should be very patient with each other I think' (80). The novel effectively enjoins such patience by situating the reader among the whole range of attempted answers to the question 'What shall I do?' in order that he or she should richly appreciate the enormous difficulty of answering that question satisfactorily in a epoch that has gone beyond great things, and where the would-be epic life must make its way in a fallen world. As social traditions gave way, and the necessity of fulfilling the role and station to which one was born gave way to the necessity of choosing that role, so the responsibilities of the individual became broader and more burdensome. As the narrator wryly points out at the opening of Chapter 9, with freedom of choice comes the possibility of making mistakes: 'And certainly, the mistakes that we male and female mortals make when we have our own way might fairly raise some wonder that we are so fond of it' (71).

Farebrother

The mistake of choosing the wrong vocation or profession is treated as a hugely serious one in *Middlemarch*, even as the novel demonstrates in the stories of Fred and Will – and especially in that of Farebrother perhaps – the extreme difficulty of finding a 'fit' between the individual inclination and a settled calling, which is also sanctioned by the myriad pressures exerted by social and personal circumstance. Farebrother's own 'fatal step' (400) in relation to vocational destiny has occurred at some point in the past. The responsibility of providing for his mother, aunt and sister compelled him to forego a passion for natural history and to enter the clergy. His living is a poor one, and since his income is inadequate to meet necessary expenditure he has been forced further to compromise his calling (beyond his natural unfitness as he sees it (170–4)) by regularly playing cards for money. Yet Farebrother's insistence upon the importance of making the right choice of profession (no one, save for Mary Garth in respect of Fred's entering the clergy, is so vehement on the matter) suggests that something more significant is at stake than mere unhappiness or poverty. When Fred tells Mr Farebrother he 'might as well go wrong' by entering the Church as any other way, Mr Farebrother remonstrates, 'That is nonsense . . . Men outlive their love, but they don't outlive the consequences of their recklessness' (506). Farebrother raises the possibility here that for a nineteenth-century man the most significant relationship is not that between himself and a woman, mediated by love, but that which exists between himself and the world, mediated by work. In the novel as a whole both 'passions' are treated as having equivalent significance:

> We are not afraid of telling over and over again how a man comes to fall in love with a woman and be wedded to her, or else be fatally parted from her . . . and are comparatively uninterested in that other kind of 'makdom and fairnesse' which must be wooed with industrious thought and patient renunciation of small desires? In the story of this passion, too, the development varies: sometimes it is the glorious marriage, sometimes frustration and final parting. (142–3)

If the responsibility for choosing the right vocation has shifted to the individual, it is the responsibility of the chosen vocation in part to fulfil the function which used to be assigned to God – that of conferring meaning and individual salvation. From this point of view, work or vocation offers the best opportunity a person has in a godless world for the kind of authentic activity that will satisfy the whole self, and redeem a human life from a crushing sense of waste and purposelessness.

Lydgate and Caleb Garth

In this respect Lydgate (as he himself put it) is one of the 'lucky' ones (163), insofar as the right vocation found him early in life. Only Caleb Garth elsewhere in the novel possesses the same certainty in relation to his professional purpose. As with Lydgate, 'the moment of vocation' had 'laid hold of his imagination in boyhood' with the force of a religious calling: 'all these sights of his youth had acted on him as poetry without the aid of poets, had made a philosophy for him without the aid of philosophers, a religion without the aid of theology' (249). But the identity between these two characters as regards their original relation to their respective callings obeys the habit of the novel as a whole in drawing attention to the great divergence in their respective destinies. Lydgate's ambition, after all, is to pursue a dual vocation – combining his clinical work as a general practitioner with scientific research, and using the former as a basis for ground-breaking enquiry into the fundaments of pathology:

'I should never have been happy in any profession that did not call forth the highest intellectual strain, and yet keep me in good warm contact with my neighbours. There is nothing like the medical profession for that: one can have the exclusive scientific life that touches the distance and befriend the old fogies in the parish too.' (163)

This is a vision of a whole life – one in which the intellectual and the practical, the mental and the physical, the general and the particular, the distant and 'warm' are all married together. Lydgate is looking for a version of what Caleb Garth has already found – a calling in which the whole self is perfectly realized: 'To do a good day's work and do it well . . . was the chief part of his own happiness' (550); 'his virtual divinities were good practical schemes, accurate work, and the faithful completion of undertakings: his prince of darkness was a slack workman' (249). 'Happiness' depends here upon the direct, unmediated relationship that exists between Caleb and his work, which makes working for him not just an expression of the self, but the self's most primary activity: he prides himself on

having 'such close contact with "business" as to get often hon-
ourably decorated with marks of dust and mortar, the damp of the
engine, or the sweet soil of the woods and fields' (ibid.).

Caleb, however, belongs to an older, simpler, socially more coherent world, in which conditions existed for the kind of settled and
harmonious relationship between man and world that Caleb represents. He is the residual example of an outmoded epic society in
which a person is what they do. Where some critics have found
sentimental nostalgia in George Eliot's treatment of Caleb Garth,
his character seems intended to embody a lost ideal relationship
between self and world which no other character in the novel
achieves to the same degree. Caleb's success is a measure of everybody else's failure, and a measure too of the problem of finding a
simple correspondence between what one is and what one does in an
age when, as George Eliot herself put it, 'the relation between within
and without becomes [every year] more baffling' (Cross, iii, 160).

Lydgate, Casaubon, Dorothea

Caleb Garth offers a model of the balance and simplicity necessary
to appreciate both the problem of vocation as it is experienced by the
other major characters, and the enormous costs of vocational failure
as they are powerfully registered in the stories of Lydgate and
Casaubon. For in these cases, as if vindicating Mr Farebrother's
warning to Fred, failure in vocation amounts to the 'tragic' failure
of a human life. Casaubon's tragedy is that he has come to the end
of a life without having completed the labour which alone would
have validated that life. Lydgate's tragedy is that, hardly yet in mid-
life, he sees that his best chance of making his life 'tell' in some meaningful way is already behind him: 'We are on a perilous margin when
we begin to look passively at our future selves, and see our own
figures led with dull consent into insipid misdoing and shabby
achievement. Poor Lydgate was inwardly groaning on that margin'
(771). Indeed, the kind of harsh question this novel forces upon its
reader is whether it is more or less tolerable to be a Casaubon facing
oblivion than a Lydgate facing the prospect of seeing through his
blighted life to the bitter end, abidingly conscious of the wreck of
his ideal. The novel's every proposition calls up its inverse or reverse.
So Lydgate's story seems brutally to realize Dorothea's 'painful
inward vision' of something to limit, direct and 'shape' her diffuse
'energies': Lydgate suffers from being cut down to size, 'shapen after

the average and fit to be packed by the gross' (143). In this novel, big (needs and ambitions) into little (life and self) both will *not* go and yet *must* go if life is to be shaped for purpose at all. Misshapenness and ill-assortment of the forms of life to inner reality is the normative pattern of the book.

MARRIAGE AND THE WOMAN QUESTION

Dorothea and Rosamond

In the Finale of the novel, the narrator asserts that 'the determining acts' of Dorothea's life – chief among them the mistake of her first marriage – 'were the mixed result of young and noble impulse struggling amidst the conditions of an imperfect social state' (821). The sentence resonates with the Prelude's characterization of the idealist young women whom Dorothea represents as 'later-born Theresas', whose 'blundering lives' are 'the offspring of a certain spiritual grandeur ill-matched with the meanness of opportunity' (3–4). Earlier versions of the novel's Finale were more specific about the extent to which these imperfections were particularly oppressive in respect of women, and it has been argued that a certain conservative timidity impelled George Eliot to understate the feminist implications of her novel.[20] There is nothing timid, however, about the rash of heavily-satirized male assumptions about the nature, capacities and role of women in the early books of the novel. For Sir James Chettam, a man's mind 'has always the advantage of being masculine . . . and even his ignorance is of a sounder quality' (21); and Sir Borthrop Trumbull asserts that 'a man whose life is of any value should think of his wife as a nurse' (310). These minor strains are echoed in the major plot lines of the novel where Casaubon believes he has found in Dorothea 'a modest young lady, with the purely appreciative, unambitious abilities of her sex' (276), while Lydgate imagines Rosamond to be the type of 'perfect womanhood . . . instructed to the true womanly limit and not a hair's breadth beyond . . . docile, therefore' (348–9).

Moreover, the two central female characters themselves represent implicit critiques of prevailing cultural and gender stereotypes. Rosamond, at one level, is the most complete victim of patriarchy, since she has in part made herself and in part been made – by her education at Mrs Lemon's school – in the image of conventional male attitudes. She possesses 'that combination of correct sentiments, music, dancing, drawing . . . and perfect blond loveliness, which made the irresistible woman for the doomed man of that date' (266), and she plays the role of ideal woman with the same kind of 'executant's instinct' (158) she brings to her piano-playing. Yet it is through Rosamond that George Eliot explodes the contemporary Victorian ideal of womanhood. Rosamond's accomplishments and refinement are achieved at the expense of trivializing her intellect and coarsening her feelings, while her exquisite manner and charm conceal an egoism and social ambition which are the antithesis of the docility she appears to represent.

Dorothea, on the other hand, is no less a victim of the patriarchal order for refusing to conform to its conventional expectations in respect of the role and behaviour of women. The consensus about women's function and capabilities in the community of Middlemarch helps to establish the crampingly oppressive milieu in which Dorothea has to try to forge a life for herself, as well as indicating how far her urgent desire to find some activity commensurate with her intellectual and emotional vitality goes against the social grain. If her 'slight regard for domestic music and feminine fine art' sets Dorothea apart from Rosamond, still, like Rosamond, she finds that her education – 'that toy-box history of the world adapted to young ladies' (84) – has unfitted her for anything other than the conventional avenues open to women of her class, those of charitable activity or marriage.

The novel in various ways underscores the degree to which such otherwise distinct women as Rosamond and Dorothea are nonetheless subject to identical socio-cultural pressures. As wives, both feel stifled by the marriages they had looked forward to, albeit with different hopes and expectations, as offering promise of fulfilment. Rosamond can no more satisfy, through matrimony, her desire for social success than Dorothea can vicariously satisfy her longing for a vocation. The novel seems deliberately to expose the great lie implicit in Victorian ideology that women could fulfil themselves and their needs through marriage and men, while realistically reproducing the conditions whereby women like Rosamond and Dorothea effectively had no 'work' but men. The fact that women's very economic survival depends on men entails the ancillary psycho-emotional problem that they have no distraction from domestic infelicity in occupation outside the home. Both Lydgate and Casaubon find solace and relief in professional pursuits or in masculine forms of play (gambling). Rosamond and Dorothea turn instead, as an alternative to the disappointment and frustration of their blighted lives, to another man, and, significantly in terms of the structural resonances of the novel, to the same man, Will Ladislaw.

Yet for all the quiet subversion of Victorian gender conventions implicit in these relationships, when Dorothea is finally united with Will, her gifts and intelligence are relegated to the role of wifely help to his reforming mission of Member of Parliament. One early reviewer felt that the sense of disappointment elicited by this betrayal of Dorothea's potential was an aspect of the novel's critique of prevailing structures: 'One feels', said R. H. Hutton '*and is probably meant to feel acutely*, that here too, it is the "meanness of opportunity" and not intrinsic suitability, which determines Dorothea's second comparatively happy marriage' (*Critical Heritage*, 306). Yet Dorothea's eventual fate has also been criticized by feminist critics as a symptom of George Eliot's ultimate acquiescence in the oppressive nineteenth-century ideal of womanhood. Dorothea is not permitted the radical steps she herself took but, instead, in finally becoming wife, guide and mother, presents renunciation and passivity as ideal virtues. Kathleen Blake has pointed out, however, that the opportunities and achievements which marriage to Will opens to Dorothea are not negligible, since his work towards political reform is an undertaking of magnitude:

> Setting the story in ante-reform times locates it in relation to the ultimate passage of reform. Dorothea helps forward a movement that would eventually prevail and that bears comparison to Saint Theresa's reform of a religious order as a 'far-resonant' action. (1983, 47)

Rosamond and Lydgate

An important consideration in this context is that marriage does not merely have political significance in this novel. Above all, marriage is presented as a great life test, in which any possibility of genuine union can seem remote or impossible, and where failures of communication between marriage partners are not susceptible to reformist-political solution.

The following paragraph (divided into sections for analysis) occurs just after Lydgate's initial attempt to enlist his wife's support in the couple's money worries (see above, Chapter 2). Lydgate now tells Rosamond that the inventory of their possessions will begin the following day:

> 'I insist upon it that your father shall not know unless I choose to tell him,' added Lydgate, with a more peremptory emphasis.
>   This certainly was unkind, but Rosamond had thrown him back on evil expectation as to what she would do in the way of quiet steady disobedience. (585)

Judgement of Lydgate, which seems as much Lydgate's criticism of himself as that of the narrator, is balanced by psychological explanation. The paragraph then shifts to register the effect of Lydgate's words on Rosamond.

> The unkindness seemed unpardonable to her: she was not given to weeping and disliked it, but now her chin and lips began to tremble and the tears welled up. (ibid.)

Rosamond, without the benefit of the narrator's psychological understanding, cannot forgive Lydgate's words as the narrator can. If this is in part a failure of imaginative sympathy on Rosamond's part, it is a failure that Lydgate also in part shares. The paragraph goes on:

> Perhaps it was not possible for Lydgate, under the double stress of outward material difficulty and of his own proud resistance to humiliating consequences, to imagine fully what this sudden trial was to a young creature who had known nothing but indulgence, and whose dreams had all been of new indulgence, more exactly to her taste. (ibid.)

The power of this passage and of the entire chapter from which it comes is its patient dramatization of the 'total missing of each another's mental track' (577), which is a tragic central failure of the Lydgate-Rosamond relationship. In obeying the formal requirements of dialogue, moving to and fro from one to the other of this couple, giving equal weight to both sides, the narration reveals that Lydgate, like Rosamond (although perhaps more excusably, given the myriad pressures besetting him) is feeling too much on his own account to 'imagine fully' what Rosamond is feeling on hers.

Often it is merely the silent gap between paragraphs which signals the extent to which these partners remain two separated worlds rather than two halves of a whole one. So when Lydgate makes his first entreaty to Rosamond:

> He laid his ample hand softly on hers, saying –
> 'Dear!' with the lingering utterance which affection gives to the word . . . 'I am obliged to tell you what will hurt you, Rosy. But there are things which husband and wife must think of together. I dare say it has occurred to you already that I am short of money.'
> Lydgate paused; but Rosamond turned her neck and looked at a vase on the mantelpiece. (584)

This is the sort of scene F. R. Leavis had in mind when he spoke of 'the sensitive precision of George Eliot's hold on dialogue' and the 'living tension' (Leavis, 94) she creates with it. Not only every word spoken but every detail of voice and movement is minutely recorded, with the effect that the force of that apparently casual connective 'but' in the final sentence is quietly devastating. The preceding semi-colon makes it possible momentarily to 'hear' the pause. It is a pause of possibility (omit the punctuation mark and Rosamond's response seems to be more immediate and spontaneous, even a reflex action) and is almost Shakespearean in the number of possible actions with which it might have been filled, and upon which Lydgate apprehensively waits, in this charged dramatic moment. Ominously, the very delay in Rosamond's response conveys all too accurately the deliberateness of her indifference to her husband's appeal.

Dorothea and Casaubon

In both central marriages of the novel, couples are brought together only to exist unfulfillingly apart. The following definitive scene occurs at the centre of the book, the close of Book Four, Chapter 42. Casaubon has just learned from Lydgate that he is dying, and Dorothea goes to join him in the garden. '[She] might have represented a heaven-sent angel coming with a promise that the short hours remaining should yet be filled with that faithful love which clings the closer to a comprehended grief':

> His glance in reply to hers was so chill that she felt her timidity increased; yet she turned and passed her hand through his arm.

Mr Casaubon kept his hands behind him and allowed her pliant arm to cling with difficulty against his rigid arm.

There was something horrible to Dorothea in the sensation which this unresponsive hardness inflicted upon her. That is a strong word, but not too strong: it is in these acts called trivialities that the seeds of joy are for ever wasted, until men and women look round with haggard faces at the devastation their own waste has made, and say, the earth bears no harvest of sweetness – calling their denial knowledge. You may ask why, in the name of manliness, Mr Casaubon should have behaved in that way. Consider that his was a mind which shrank from pity: have you ever watched in such a mind the effect of a suspicion that what is pressing it as a grief may be really a source of contentment, either actual or future, to the being who already offends by pitying? Besides, he knew little of Dorothea's sensations, and had not reflected that on such an occasion as the present they were comparable in strength to his own sensibilities about Carp's criticisms. (419–20)

Again, minute attention, in the first two sentences, to what is going on at the surface level of look and touch is supported, as the scene develops, by scrupulously incisive disclosure of what exists around or beneath or is implicit within those modes. What the passage as a whole discloses, as it imaginatively inhabits now Dorothea's, now Casaubon's experience of the moment, is how these two are inadvertently hurting one another out of the equivalent sense of hurt they are suffering within themselves. The initial paragraph division – a Dorothea paragraph, then a Casaubon paragraph – bears silent witness to the fact that neither Dorothea nor Casaubon can cross the boundary of being that separates them as easily as the author-narrator can. Together in marriage, together in the moment, they are doomed to suffer the unhappiness and mutual failure of their relationship alone.

Even the effort of sympathy which does go out from Dorothea to Casaubon remains entirely and uselessly separate from him: 'Mr Casaubon kept his hands behind him and allowed her pliant arm to cling with difficulty against his rigid arm.' At such times, it is these failures in communication between her characters which seem to bring the narrator, as a voice or articulating presence, into being. Summoned as that voice characteristically is by what remains unexpressed inside or between people, George Eliot, as narrator, is here occupying the gap in understanding that exists between Dorothea and Casaubon, and saying on their behalf what they cannot say to themselves or to one another. George Eliot often seems to exist within her novels to give tangible reality and articulate presence to feelings and thoughts which often cannot be acknowledged by humans themselves, yet which call for articulation in others if their human meaning is not to be wasted, lost or forgotten amid life's relative density. Such verbal recognition, as the novel repeatedly confirms, is perhaps all that can be offered by way of alleviation of the human problems it unfolds. Back in the test of ordinary living, a Casaubon would resist the imaginative sympathy the narrator extends, as completely as he shuns Dorothea's: 'Consider that his was a mind which shrank from pity.'

The sense of separation from her husband seems as final as the separation death itself will shortly bring: 'Like one who has lost his way and is weary . . . she saw her own and her husband's solitude – how they walked apart' (421). Yet before Book Four, and Casaubon's life, finally closes, there is an unexpected counter-movement. Resolving to try to ease her husband's suffering, Dorothea waits for him as he leaves the library to retire to rest:

'Dorothea!' he said, with a gentle surprise in his tone. 'Were you waiting for me?'

'Yes, I did not like to disturb you.'

'Come, my dear, come. You are young, and need not to extend your life by watching.'

When the kind quiet melancholy of that speech fell on Dorothea's ears, she felt something like the thankfulness that might well up in us if we had narrowly escaped hurting a lamed creature. She put her hand into her husband's, and they went along the broad corridor together. (422)

The final sentence recalls the close of Milton's *Paradise Lost* as Adam and Eve, 'hand in hand, with wandering steps and slow', leave Eden. Milton's concluding words are remembered once more as *Middlemarch*'s own epic narrative comes to its close in the novel's Finale:

Marriage, which has been the bourne of so many narratives, is still a great beginning, as it was to Adam and Eve, who kept their honeymoon in Eden, but had their first little one among the thorns and thistles of the wilderness. It is still the beginning of the home epic – the gradual conquest or irremediable loss of that complete union which makes the advancing years a climax, and age the harvest of sweet memories in common. (815)

Marriage is indeed, in this novel, the place or condition in which its creatures discover the essential, perhaps final loneliness of separated consciousness; and this discovery, the Miltonic allusion suggests, is an inescapable symptom of human fallenness. In *Middlemarch* the calamity of the fall, as well as the tiny human gestures which either repeat it (in Rosamond's case) or compensate and partially atone for it (in Dorothea's and Casaubon's), are dispersed across the marital couplings of provincial-domestic, rather than epic, life.

IDEALISM AND REALISM

In *Middlemarch*, 'the rhetoric of social hopefulness is everywhere; one cannot turn a page without reading of notions, schemes, reforms and plans'. Talk of model farm, model hospitals, colonies of workers' cottages and scientific farming runs throughout the novel, and in characters as otherwise diverse as Sir James Chettam and Caleb Garth. It is as if the 'vast and inchoate yearning for the good' initiated by a secular age has been 'broken down and distributed among the multitude of fictional forms that populate the novel' (Mintz, 62–3). Dorothea is offered as a prototype of this phenomenon. Her own 'yearning for the good' is one of the first things we learn about her, and she speaks movingly for a central and defining experience of the novel when she says to Lydgate in their conversation over the hospital in Chapter 44:

'How happy you must be, to know things that you feel sure will do great good! I wish I could awake with that knowledge every morning. There seems to be so much trouble taken that one can hardly see the good of!' (434)

For a novel so concerned with its characters' need to originate or generate some benefit in the life of humankind, the examples of success are rare indeed. As we have seen, so much of this novel is concerned with the urge materially to alter a world that is resistingly

intent upon defining the individual. These oppositional forces sometimes emerge as the explicit subject matter of the leading pioneers of
reform, so that the reader both witnesses the phenomenon of these
oppositional forces and hears characters discussing them in way
which, as with the operation of the narrative voice, adds another rich
layer or dimension.

Lydgate and Ladislaw

The analogous nature of the situations of Lydgate and Ladislaw is
emphasized by the structural placing, back to back (Chapters 45 and
46), of their respective reformist activities. The discussion between
the two, at the close of Chapter 46, about ways and means of achiev-
ing reform is a brilliant example of the novel's method of discrimi-
nating illuminating difference in broad, even close, similarity.

Their disagreement centres on the suitability or otherwise of Mr
Brooke as a parliamentary candidate on the reformist side. Judging
from his record to date as a reforming landlord and as a director of
the hospital, Lydgate insists: 'He's not fit to be a public man . . . He
would disappoint everybody who counted on him.' 'That depends
on how you fix your standard of public men', Will counters. 'He's
good enough for the occasion.' Ladislaw opposes a pragmatic view
– 'whether we are to try for nothing till we find immaculate men to
work with' – to Lydgate's purist, principled stance. Yet Ladislaw's
pragmatism itself rests upon a point of principle:

> 'Wait for wisdom and conscience in public agents – fiddlestick!
> The only conscience we can trust to is the massive sense of wrong
> in a class, and the best wisdom that will work is the wisdom of
> balancing claims. That's my test – which side is injured? I support
> the man who supports their claims; not the virtuous upholder of
> the wrong.' (458–9)

Ladislaw forsakes the ideal candidate – a man of 'wisdom and conscience' – for the higher ideal of attempting to set to right a massive
social wrong, even thereby risking his own integrity (since his
support for Brooke involves his 'puffing' the man in his political
journalism so as to disguise the man's defects). Ladislaw's position
appears to be endorsed by the epigraph to the chapter ('Since we
cannot get what we like, let us like what we can get') and by the developing dialogue itself. Ladislaw goes on:

'If there were one man who would carry you a medical reform and another who would oppose it, should you inquire which had the better motives or even the better brains?'

'Oh, of course,' said Lydgate, seeing himself checkmated by a move which he had often used himself, 'if one did not work with such men as are at hand, things must come to a dead-lock.' (458–60)

Pragmatism was, of course, Lydgate's own unofficial and uncomfortable position when he voted for Tyke against Farebrother; and here it comes as an inadvertent proof of the difficulty of any person reliably embodying honourable principle. Conversations of this kind imitate the novel's own fluidity in turning ideas inside-out and back again. These shifts of focus happen simply by virtue of time and the sentences going on.

Dorothea and Farebrother

In his explicit recognition of the need for compromise and of the difficulty of translating absolute principles into action, Ladislaw, it has been argued, is closely allied with his creator: 'Ladislaw, like the realist novelist, asserts the complicating energies of a "mixed" reality as he attempts to change it, through language, which is the medium of the ideal.'[21] Inside the language of the realist novel, Ladislaw is also in this respect closer to a youthful, and more ambitious and successful version, of Mr Farebrother than of Mr Brooke (thus seemingly endless are the possibilities of comparison and contrast in this novel). Mr Farebrother's entire life is a compromise: between the duties and conduct demanded by his profession, the economic imperatives that drive him to play cards for money; and between the vocation, as natural scientist, he had wanted, and the career he has been forced to follow. 'Like Lydgate in the last pages of the novel, Farebrother lives in the shadow of the missed opportunity but . . . has more balance and less intensity than Lydgate, [because] he has come to terms with Middlemarch and almost with himself.'[22] On this reading, Farebrother is a character who represents 'the middle way' of equable acceptance of individual limitation apparently endorsed not only by the fates of the idealists in the novel, but by the novel's title.

Once again, as in the example above, a significantly placed dialogue, late in the novel, sets the definitive Farebrother balance 'in play'. The conversation between Dorothea and Farebrother that opens the final book of the novel concerns how to act in respect of Lydgate when, after the death of the blackmailer Raffles, the doctor is suspected of having accepted money as a bribe from the now disgraced banker, Bulstrode. 'I cannot be indifferent to the troubles of a man who advised me in *my* trouble', Dorothea says. 'What do we live for, if it is not to make life less difficult to each other?' Dorothea's 'impetuous genorosity', as the narrator terms it, undergoes a 'melancholy check' when she comes to 'consider all the circumstances of the case by the light of Mr Farebrother's experience'. This first sentence of the opening chapter of the final book of the novel might lead us to expect a clinching example of the dialogue between youthful idealism and experienced realism which has gone on throughout the novel, since Farebrother first warned Lydgate of the 'old Adam' or since Dorothea's aspirations were first ironized by the narrator in Chapter 1. In the case of Dorothea, Lydgate, Ladislaw, Fred, Casaubon, Bulstrode, Rosamond and Mr Brooke, ideals in the areas of marriage or of profession have been baulked or renounced, and all have had to face the realization which comes (thus terribly to Lydgate) that 'life must be taken up on a lower stage of expectation, as it is by men who have lost their limbs' (641). Amid this sense of waste, Farebrother has offered a benign, consolatory, even redeeming representative of mature realism in the face of an attenuated life. In this spirit, Farebrother advises Dorothea that Lydgate's friends 'must wait till they find an opportunity' to act on his behalf:

'It is possible – I have often felt so much weakness in myself that I can conceive even a man of honourable disposition, such as I have always believed Lydgate to be, succumbing to such a temptation as that of accepting money which was offered more or less indirectly as a bribe to insure his silence about scandalous facts long gone by. I say, I can conceive this, if he were under the pressure of hard circumstances – if he had been harassed as I feel sure Lydgate has been. I would not believe anything worse of him except under stringent proof. But there is the terrible Nemesis following on some errors, that it is always possible for those who like it to interpret them into a crime: there is no proof in favour of the man outside his own consciousness and assertion.'

'Oh, how cruel!' said Dorothea, clasping her hands. 'And would you not like to be the one person who believed in that man's innocence, if the rest of the world belied him? Besides, there is the man's character beforehand to speak for him.'

'But, my dear Mrs Casaubon,' said Mr Farebrother, smiling gently at her ardour, 'character is not cut in marble – it is not something solid and unalterable. It is something living and changing, and may become diseased as our bodies do.'

'Then it may be rescued and healed,' said Dorothea. 'I should not be afraid of asking Mr Lydgate to tell me the truth, that I might help him. Why should I be afraid? . . . I might . . . take [Mr Bulstrode's] place in providing for the Hospital; and I have to consult Mr Lydgate, to know thoroughly what are the prospects of doing good by keeping up the present plans. This is the best opportunity in the world for me to ask for his confidence; and he would be able to tell me things which might make all the circumstances clear. Then we would all stand by him and bring him out of his trouble. People glorify all sorts of bravery except the bravery they might show on behalf of their nearest neighbours.' Dorothea's eyes had a moist brightness in them, and the changed tones of her voice roused her uncle, who began to listen.

'It is true that a woman may venture on some efforts of sympathy which would hardly succeed if men undertook them,' said Mr Farebrother, almost converted by Dorothea's ardour. (724–5)

Farebrother's sane commonsense in having only moderate expectation of Lydgate's honour is offered as strong currency here. His wisdom rests in part on his more intimate knowledge of Lydgate's recent desperation, his gambling in particular; his gentle smile at Dorothea's ardour recalls the narrator's only delicate ironizing of Dorothea's idealism in Book One; and his pronouncement on character as 'not cut in marble' but 'living and changing' (often quoted non-contextually as the narrator's own judgement) seems upheld by the shape of individual stories within the novel, thus enforcing a sense of Farebrother's authority as the author-narrator's surrogate. But that narratorial voice is now put in dialogue, as it were, with Dorothea's own, to the effect that there are powerful counter-suggestions: that Farebrother is judging Lydgate rather too much by his own sense of limitation, frustrations and compromise ('I have often felt so much weakness in myself'); that his resultant caution in relation to Lydgate's situation is ungenerous, even faintly cowardly, beside Dorothea's determination to believe in Lydgate's innocence, and to act on that belief at once. Indeed it is Dorothea's ardent belief in Lydgate's innocence that propels her into *finding* the opportunity which Farebrother has cautioned her to wait for: ' "This is the best opportunity in the world . . ." ' It is as if idealism is actually producing pragmatism here in the form of an opportunistic practical plan. The narration, moreover, is noticeably unironic about how the conviction with which Dorothea asserts her ideal has a real, palpable effect on those around her: her uncle 'began to listen', Mr Farebrother is 'almost converted'.

F. R. Leavis famously explained the value put upon Dorothea's idealism at such times as the result of the author's uncritical indulgence of her heroine. For Leavis, the sympathetic portrayal of Dorothea's idealistic ardour – like her exalted religious enthusiasms and the associations with St Theresa and the Virgin Mary – are symptomatic of the author's own 'soul-hunger' and 'unqualified self-identification' with her heroine. (Leavis, 75). For Laurence Lerner, Leavis's criticism was more ethical than artistic: 'Valuing the Theresa-complex [the desire to do some active good] less than George Eliot does and maturity more, [Leavis] has passed off his ethical disagreement, as if it were the discovery of an artistic flaw.'[23] George Eliot's own ethical valuing of Dorothea's idealism is registered in the narratorial comment which accompanies Dorothea's conclusion that much of her own income and inheritance rightfully belongs to Will Ladislaw, and is preparing to broach the subject with Mr Casaubon:

> She was blind, you see, to many things obvious to others – likely to tread in the wrong places, as Celia had warned her; yet her blindness to whatever did not lie in her own pure purpose carried her safely by the side of precipices where vision would have been perilous with fear. (369)

Sometimes, this passage suggests, it is morally 'safer' *not* to possess the mature wisdom that sees in advance all the possible results or effects of an action, since innocence of these effects leaves a person free to do the right thing, purely and uncompromisingly, regardless of what might be the personal consequences. And Dorothea's instinct proves right to the degree that in her interview with Lydgate, her belief in his character enables him to recover, perhaps for the last time, the 'wholeness' of it (751). In a world of lost absolutes, it still pays to be absolutist at times, and that is offered as a kind of novelistic surprise or discovery. This is a novel which continually and fearlessly tests its own propositions and dispositions, such that in the conversation discussed above the narratorial, worldly-wise authority which reigned supreme in Book One now finds itself faintly worsted as the novel draws to its close.

EGOISM

A novel that rested upon a belief in the capacity for fellow-feeling is also the most profound study of the kinds of individual egoism which are an obstacle to such imaginative sympathy. The novel's most famous pronouncement on this limitation is expressed imagistically and 'scientifically':

> An eminent philosopher among my friends, who can dignify even your ugly furniture by lifting it into the serene light of science, has shown me this pregnant little fact. Your pier-glass or extensive surface of polished steel made to be rubbed by a housemaid, will be minutely and multitudinously scratched in all directions; but place now against it a lighted candle as a centre of illumination, and lo! the scratches will seem to arrange themselves in a fine series of concentric circles round that little sun. It is demonstrable that the scratches are going everywhere impartially, and it is only your candle which produces the flattering illusion of a concentric arrangement, its light falling with an exclusive optical selection. These things are a parable. The scratches are events, and the candle is the egoism of any person now absent – of Miss Vincy, for example. (261–2)

While each individual inhabits what seems to him or her to be a 'centre' – his or her own consciousness – that centre is in fact 'only' (an innocently terrible word in this context) the 'flattering illusion' produced by self-absorption. Moreover, that apparent centre, most dizzyingly of all perhaps, is only *one* among infinite possible centres (those of 'any' other person) where personal egoism operates to render individually meaningful, events which are intrinsically 'impartial' and arbitrary. The use of scientific and religious discourse together suggest that this law is at once ancient and empirically provable: the phenomenon will hold true at every repetition of the experiment. The experimental lives of this novel, moreover, validate that law. The 'parable' seems to offer, even from within the novel, a non-novelistic, clinically objective explanation of the fates of the characters as creatures subject less to deterministic plot than to necessary human laws.

At the same time the pier-glass is an intrinsic part of the rich imagistic life of this novel, and helps to show how its 'condensed', 'compacted' (Beer, 1986, 192–3) imagery works. Windows, mirrors and reflective images abound within the novel, as we saw at the opening of this chapter. Characteristically, they express a narcissistic gaze that is turned inward upon the self rather than outward upon the world. (In Dorothea, this distortion or inadequacy of vision is accompanied by her literal short-sightedness.) At one level, the optical image, apparently targeting Rosamond, draws together, as if centripetally, disparate examples of egoistic tendencies that precede it in the formal sequencing of the novel:

> Dorothea by this time had looked deep into the ungauged reservoir of Mr Casaubon's mind, seeing reflected there in vague labyrinthine extension every quality she herself brought. (23)

> Fred fancied that he saw to the bottom of his uncle Featherstone's soul, though in reality half what he saw there was no more than the reflexion of his own inclinations. (117)

Conversely, a latent centrifugal energy is activated as soon as subsequent examples implicitly claim the significance of the image to themselves, and make its target the character and reader at once. On Mr Casaubon's inability to see anything but suppressed rebellion and judgement of his failures even in Dorothea's offers of wifely love, the narrator comments: 'Will not a tiny speck very close to our vision blot out the glory of the world, and leave only a margin by which we see the blot? I know no speck as troublesome as self' (413). To any temptation on the reader's part to feel superior to Casaubon by virtue of sharing in the narrator's understanding of him, comes, in that sharp second sentence, an austere reminder of the pier-glass law. This is a point where the depth-charge sent into the narrative by the pier-glass image and the cumulative resonance of related images might or might not detonate according to the size of the reader's own 'blot'. The troublesome 'self' is not simply synonymous with 'ego' here, but with everything the ego recognizes as conferring a meaningful life. On the issue of Mr Bulstrode's religious hypocrisy, the narrator comments:

> This was not what Mr Bulstrode said to any man for the sake of deceiving him: it was what he said to himself – it was as genuinely his mode of explaining events as any theory of yours may be, if you happen to disagree with him. For the egoism which enters into our theories does not affect their sincerity; rather, the more our egoism is satisfied, the more robust is our belief. (513)

One of the compacted, complicating meanings of the pier-glass image is unpacked here in the startling twist of that final sentence. It is impossible to dismiss as mere deluded solipsism an operation of the ego that is both a measure and a guarantee of sincerity and belief. The experimental proof is there in Dorothea, and especially in Lydgate. The speck that blots out the rest of humanity in an order of being constituted as Casaubon's is, becomes, in a Lydgate, an aid to heroic efforts of humanistic altruism.

Bulstrode and Rosamond
Yet almost no major character escapes the moment which, as we saw with Dorothea in Chapters 1 and 2, 'ends the dream of self, which marks the rude and salutary awakening to the world, where self is reduced'.[24] Casaubon's egoism remains its own punishment: 'It is an uneasy lot at best, to be . . . present at this great spectacle of life and never to be liberated from a small hungry shivering self' (277). The fearful self-protectiveness which insulates him from the scrutiny of the world turns into the isolation and loneliness from which he suffers. Yet Casaubon's is a self so immersed in its own unease as to be unable even to begin to get the measure of the catastrophe it represents. The loss of the dream of self in Rosamond and in Bulstrode, by contrast, comes as a terrible Nemesis:

> Rosamond, while [Will's] poisoned weapons were being hurled at her . . . seemed to be waking into some new terrible existence. She had no sense of chill resolute repulsion, of reticent self-justification such as she had known under Lydgate's most stormy displeasure; all her sensibility was turned into a bewildering novelty of pain; she felt a new terrified recoil under a lash never experienced before. (767)

The quick vision that his life was after all a failure, that he was a dishonoured man . . . the sense of utter futility in that equivocation with his conscience in dealing with the life of his accomplice, an equivocation which now turned venomously upon him with the full-grown fang of a discovered lie: – all this rushed through him like the agony of terror which fails to kill, and leaves the ears still open to the returning wave of execration. (715–16)

Where Rosamond is crushed by the sudden pressure of a world beyond the self, Bulstrode is cruelly visited by the appalling knowledge of what lies within. The language is terrifyingly physical. The discarded conscience for which, as we saw in Chapter 1, George Eliot's language even sympathetically substituted, has sharpened fatally and suicidally into that venomous 'full-grown fang'. For Rosamond, the shattering truth comes like a breach in flesh itself: 'What another nature felt in opposition to her own was being burnt and bitten into her consciousness' (767). In Bulstrode, as in Rosamond, the sense of the world as a malleable extension of self has been absolute. The hard reality, which they have refused to see or deliberately evaded, now avenges itself upon them, not just toppling the self's supremacy but virtually annihilating any sense of self at all: '[she] was almost losing the sense of her identity' (ibid.); 'all this rushed through him like the agony of terror which fails to kill'.

The violence of the fall when it comes is a measure of the extent to which, under the terms of this novel's cosmology, Rosamond and Bulstrode need to have forced upon them the knowledge that they will not, or cannot, see for themselves. If the capacity for human fellowship offered for George Eliot 'the humanistic equivalent of, and replacement for, the Christian conception of grace' (McSweeney, 27), it follows that the 'moral stupidity' exhibited in all her creatures to some degree is analogous to the Christian doctrine of original sin, the inherited condition of mortality. These moments of awakening in Rosamond and Bulstrode are a secular version of the scourge of the old Adam, which at the same time help to reveal and to clarify why Dorothea's emergence from moral stupidity in Chapter 22, by contrast, is a moment of grace. Mere sensitivity is not at issue here, since in Bulstrode the experience increases sensibility's power: 'The sudden sense of exposure after the re-established sense of safety came – not to the coarse organisation of a criminal but – to the susceptible nerve of a man whose intensest being lay in such mastery and predominance as the conditions of his life had shaped for him' (716). The difference is that Bulstrode still sees only himself and a divinity that has let him down: 'God had disowned him before men and left him unscreened to the triumphant scorn of those who were glad to have their hatred justified' (715). Dorothea's distinction, even uniqueness, in this novel is her capacity to recognize her husband as a separate, equivalent centre, and survive that recognition even as the accepting realization of mutual equivalence leaves her alone in stranded separateness.

RELIGION

When in Chapter 50 Dorothea begins to consider choosing Farebrother over Bulstrode's protégé, Mr Tyke ('a zealous, able man' of 'fervent intention', (183)) as successor to the living at Lowick, she states her reason thus:

> 'I have always been thinking of the different ways in which Christianity is taught, and whenever I find one that makes it a wider blessing than any other, I cling to that as the truest – I mean that which takes in the most good of all kinds, and brings in the most people as sharers in it. It is surely better to pardon too much than to condemn too much.' (488–9)

Dorothea makes explicit here a view of formal religion that is implicit in the novel as a whole. The teachings of the church and the clergy are not irrelevant and valueless in a godless world. On the contrary, they are to be cherished where they foster a sense of human fellowship and community, as Farebrother's teaching does in a literal sense. ('People outside his parish went to hear him,' we are told, at a time when 'to fill the church was the most difficult part of a clergyman's function.' (75)) Farebrother's 'wider', more tolerant and inclusive teaching is most directly opposed in *Middlemarch* to that of Bulstrode, in whom George Eliot exposes the self-serving essence of the Calvinist Evangelicalism to which she herself was committed in her youth. Mr Vincy's contempt for Bulstrode's wish 'to play bishop and banker everywhere' (129), and Mr Farebrother's dislike of Bulstrode's 'worldly-spiritual cliquism' ('they really look on the rest of mankind as a doomed carcases which is to nourish them for heaven', (173)), enforces the relationship between Bulstrode's economic entrepreneurialism and his evangelical faith long before his criminal corruption is brought to light. His zeal for business and religion are self-interestedly motivated by a desire for, respectively, power and influence in this world and personal salvation in the next. Indeed, one success leads to the other, since Bulstrode interprets all his financial triumphs as evidence of divine favour and as sanction of his improper business practices: 'God's cause was something distinct from his own rectitude of conduct: it enforced a discrimination of God's enemies, who were to be used merely as instruments, and whom it would be well . . . to keep out of money and consequent influence' (610). The Evangelical encouragement to belief in an implacable deity who is only to be appeased by acts that visibly resound to His glory fosters the excessive concern with self and salvation at the expense of others that the narrator calls 'the religion of personal fear'. It is a religion, the narrator goes on, echoing Farebrother's predatory image, 'which remains at the level of the savage' (611). Bulstrode's corrupt self-designation as 'God's servant' finds its correction in Farebrother, who by modestly making it his duty to be 'only a parson among parishioners whose lives he has to try and make better' (488) preserves what is best in the Christian tradition for a secular world by humanizing its teaching.

Yet Farebrother is also implicitly contrasted with Casaubon and Fred as models of less 'Christian' forms of secularization within the clergy. 'His being a clergyman', Mary says of Fred, 'would be only for gentility's sake . . . he would be a piece of professional affectation . . . a caricature' (509). When the role of clergyman has become a mere profession, the form of Christianity has priority over the content – the wrong way round for George Eliot who believed, with Feuerbach, in the necessity of the modern world's retaining the content of Christianity whatever the inevitability of its formal apparatus disappearing. If Mr Brooke is a type of Will Ladislaw projected into the future, then Mr Cadwallader, the Rector, is a version of what Fred, as clergyman, might have been – a man whose 'conscience was large and easy like the rest of him: it did only what it could do without any trouble' (70). Yet the particular species of 'genteel' Christianity that the Cadwalladers represent is by no means a mere 'caricature', and its benefits to the community are analogous to those offered by Farebrother, 'giving a neighbourliness to both rank and religion' (51). Mr Cadwallader's judicious generosity of spirit makes him a foil in his turn to Mr Casaubon, who has translated his divine office into a worldly pursuit in ways that recall

Mr Bulstrode. As his search for the 'Key to all Mythologies' has more or less replaced his clerical calling, so the community of scholarly critics whose scorn he fears has largely taken the place of a divine authority in Casaubon's system of belief. The world and its good opinion have replaced the idea of God, and Casaubon suffers as much as his flock from this substitution of egoistic for religious ends. As Alan Mintz has pointed out, the message of this novel with regard to the clergy seems to be that if the role cannot be humanized it should be avoided altogether.

Dorothea
The authentic religion in *Middlemarch* is the informally, personally evolved form which Dorothea embodies. In Chapter 80, Dorothea completes the journey which began at the advent of her adult life when she first arrived at Lowick and sought a 'sense of connection with a manifold pregnant existence'. In order to become part of that existence, Dorothea must undergo a version of the dark night of the soul:

> In that hour she repeated what the merciful eyes of solitude have looked on for ages in the spiritual struggles of man – she besought hardness and coldness and aching weariness to bring her relief from the mysterious incorporeal might of her anguish: she lay on the bare floor and let the night grow cold around her; while her grand woman's frame was shaken by sobs as if she had been a despairing child. (773–4)

A woman, 'discover[ing] her passion to herself in the unshrinking utterance of despair' (ibid.), admits her love for a man whom she now believes to love another. The situation is 'not unusual'; the circumstances are hardly great or heroic. Yet George Eliot places this struggle unhesitatingly in a great tradition of the 'spiritual struggles of men'; only the 'merciful eyes of solitude' now replace those of God, leaving Dorothea like 'An infant crying in the night:/. . .And with no language but a cry' (Tennyson, *In Memoriam*, LIV). It is the utter absence of help in this situation which renders the outcome of her struggle a form of religious heroism:

> She opened her curtains, and looked out towards the bit of road that lay in view, with fields beyond, outside the entrance-gates. On the road there was a man with a bundle on his back and a woman

carrying her baby; in the field she could see figures moving –
perhaps the shepherd with his dog. Far off in the bending sky was
the pearly light; and she felt the largeness of the world and the
manifold wakings of men to labour and endurance. She was a
part of that involuntary, palpitating life, and could neither look
out on it from her luxurious shelter as a mere spectator, nor hide
her eyes in selfish complaining. (776)

The 'manifold' 'largeness of the world' has no longer to be 'kept up
painfully as an inward vision'. It is what she sees when she looks out
of the window, where she is herself now a figure in the vision. The
hope that this man and woman seen beneath the sky give to
Dorothea 'comes not as a gift but almost as a rebuke'; if Dorothea
is 'a part of that involuntary, palpitating life', still she is only 'a *part*'
of it. The vision is won at the cost of Dorothea's fullest recognition
of her own littleness in relation to the world's largeness. Her achievement is not sudden conversion, but the finding of a 'middle way'
that is not merely the way of compromise: 'Between two negative
extremes ('neither as mere spectator', 'nor in selfish complaining')
[Dorothea] manages to sustain a vision which is itself not negative . . . [It] loosens the hold of ideas of solitude and failure, and
stands in place of the idea of God, keeping humans within this life
for their meanings' (Davis, 1983, 321–2). At this critical moment,
where her spiritual struggle is translated into an effort to 'save'
Rosamond, Dorothea embodies an immanent, as opposed to tran-
scendent or merely formal, faith – a belief that humanity's final
meaning and hope is to be found within life, not outside or above it.
   It is in these terms that we should read the Finale, where Dorothea
is left with the 'feeling that there was always something better which
she might have done, if she had only been better and known better',
and where:

Many who knew her, thought it a pity that so substantive and rare
a creature should have been absorbed into the life of another, and
be only known in a certain circle as a wife and mother. But no one
stated exactly what else was in her power she ought rather to have
done. (819)

Of course, 'the conditions of an imperfect social state' and
specifically of a woman's position within it are answerable here. But

the stronger emphasis is that there is no recognized vocation that could have channelled or 'shaped' such 'power'. In *Middlemarch* as a whole, the kind of goodness that Dorothea represents has no distinct or settled vocation. 'I am not a model clergyman – only a decent makeshift', says Mr Farebrother (174). Moreover, the greatest occasions of human goodness in the novel are of a deeply uncongenial, inconvenient and involuntary kind, the sort of calling no one would willingly choose. Farebrother intercedes with Mary Garth on Fred's behalf, even though he loves Mary himself; Lydgate supports Bulstrode as he collapses, even though this compromises him utterly, and destroys his reputation and career. In both cases professional ethics support but do not determine the performance of what is felt to be a human duty.

In Dorothea's case, a recognizably Spinozan form of 'energetic action' produces the decision in relation to Rosamond in Chapter 80:

> All the active thought with which she had before been representing to herself the trials of Lydgate's lot, and this marriage union which, like her own, seemed to have its hidden as well as evident troubles – all this vivid sympathetic experience returned to her now as a power: it asserted itself as acquired knowledge asserts itself and will not let us see as we saw in the day of our ignorance. She said to her own irremediable grief, that it should make her more helpful, instead of driving her back from effort. (775)

The conversion of feeling to clear-eyed knowledge that has the 'power' to do good in the world almost exactly reproduces the Spinozan sequence whereby inadequate or confused ideas (Spinoza's definition of emotion) are counteracted by adequate ideas that release a person into acting in place of suffering. Such conversion produces converts, too. Rosamond's 'generous effort' in 'redeeming [Dorothea] from suffering' is 'a reflex of [Dorothea's] own energy' (785); a species of this 'reflex energy' moves Fred Vincy 'quite newly' when Mr Farebrother (thus sacrificing his own hopes of happiness) warns him that he is on his way to losing Mary's love by slipping into bad (gambling) habits: '[A fine act] produces a sort of regenerating shudder through the frame and makes one feel ready to begin a new life. A good degree of that effect was just then present in Fred Vincy' (666). In demonstrating the 'saving influence . . . the divine efficacy of rescue that may lie in a self-subduing act of fellowship' (789), such moments seem to make visible how 'the growing good of the world is partly dependent on unhistoric acts' (Finale, 822). Yet one big realist achievement of this novel is that these small human acts, even as they reveal the highest human virtues, remain caught within the restricted prosaic medium of provincial life, subordinated in situation and circumstance. The Finale refuses to provide the dramatic release from the smallness of life that life characteristically does not deliver. In the finest chapters of this novel, life's greatness is discovered embedded in its texture.

'Unhistoric acts': Mrs Bulstrode

In Chapter 74, arriving home having learned of her husband's disgrace, Mrs Bulstrode 'locked herself in her room. She needed time to get used to her maimed consciousness, her poor lopped life, before she could walk steadily to the place allotted her'. In the immediately succeeding paragraph, we are told:

> She knew, when she locked her door, that she should unlock it ready to go down to her unhappy husband and espouse his sorrow, and say of his guilt, I will mourn and not reproach. But she needed time to gather up her strength; she needed to sob out her farewell to all the gladness and pride of her life. When she had resolved to go down, she prepared herself by some little acts which might seem mere folly to a hard onlooker . . . (739)

In the time-out allowed by the locked room, Mrs Bulstrode finds the strength to commit herself to her 'lopped' future life, and even – in embracing humiliation and 'espousing' his sorrow – to 're-marry' Bulstrode, as if what really happens here is a hidden and lonely playing out of the marriage service. Mrs Bulstrode's 'little acts' contain within them, subterraneously, very big things, the clue to which here is the word 'prepared'. It is Lydgate who recognizes that great works are 'prepared' microscopically by tiny phenomena, and in the sentences that intervene between the repetition of 'she needed time', the prose discloses the minute process by which Mrs Bulstrode finds the power within herself to fulfil her commitment:

> She could not judge him leniently: the twenty years in which she had believed in him and venerated him by virtue of his

concealments came back with particulars that made them seem an odious deceit. He had married her with that bad past life hidden behind him and she had no faith left to protest his inno-cence . . . But this imperfectly-taught woman . . . had a loyal spirit within her. (ibid.)

As judgement replaces belief, so loyalty replaces 'faith'. An appar-ently minute distinction expresses the chasm that exists between the life she is leaving behind and the one she is walking 'steadily' towards. Loyalty, like Dorothea's pity for Casaubon, is second-best, and what becomes of belief and love when those primary things are no longer possible. Thus, there is nothing merely conventionally 'loyal' in Mrs Bulstrode's resolve to go down to her husband. It is a brave act of piety. But it is a great act performed by an imperfect, rather dull woman who requires the support of those 'little acts' of ritual: taking off her ornaments and putting on a plain gown and bonnet 'which made her look suddenly like an early Methodist' (740).

The prose recalls this unwonted religious aura a paragraph or so later, when Mrs Bulstrode approaches her husband and says, 'Look up, Nicholas' (ibid.), as if in secular imitation of the Bible's 'Look up, and lift up your heads; for your redemption draweth nigh' (Luke 21:28). But in *Middlemarch* there is no redemption. There is forgive-ness, but only of a compromised kind. 'She could not say, "How much is only slander and false suspicion?" and he did not say, "I am innocent." ' (740). Those words end the chapter in this world of no happy endings. Yet something is achieved here. 'There is a forsaking', the narrator remarks early in the passage 'which still sits at the same board and lies on the same couch with the forsaken soul, with-ering it the more by unloving proximity' (739). This is not so much a didactic generalization as a memory: we think of Rosamond when Lydgate says, of their money troubles, that they must 'think together': 'Lydgate paused; but Rosamond turned her neck and looked at a vase on the mantelpiece' (584). It is one of those 'acts called trivialities' (420) that gives retrospective meaning to Dorothea's apparently useless gesture in relation to Casaubon: 'His glance in reply to hers was so chill that she felt her timidity increased; *yet she turned* and passed her hand through his arm' (420, my emphasis). The ecology of the novel reclaims such moments, even as they make nothing better, as not merely redundant or wasted but as worthwhile, for promising something better in the ecology of the world beyond the novel. So, too, when Mr and Mrs Bulstrode are brought together in one sentence in the final paragraph of the chapter, what happens helps in its small saint-like way to redeem those earlier failures: 'He burst out crying and they cried together, she sitting at his side' (740). In the syntax of the Dorothea-Casaubon marriage, the second part of that sentence would have been 'and she cried too'. But Mrs Bulstrode's separate reasons for crying are here absorbed into the constancy of weeping 'together' with her husband. What Dorothea cannot do for Casaubon, what Rosamond will not do for Lydgate, Mrs Bulstrode does do for her husband. Mrs Bulstrode is no perfect saviour. She saves her marriage not the world. But even in its very closeness to failure, this patched-up marriage, with its near-view of death, preserves a memory of what is possible for the race.

NOTES

1 Barbara Hardy, 'The Moment of Disenchantment in George Eliot's Novels' in Creeger, 61, 64–5.
2 The most recent relevant study can be found in Barbara Hardy, 'The Woman at the Window' in Patricia Gately, Dennis Leavens and D. Cole Woodcox (eds) (1997) *Perspectives on Self and Community*. Lampeter: Edwin Mellen Press.
3 Elizabeth Deeds Ermarth uses the term 'growing-points' for 'moments of encounter between one system of intelligibility and another' in Rignall (1997), 40.
4 For discussion of his passage in relation to G. H. Lewes's and Spinoza's thinking on mind and body see Davis (2006), 40–1.
5 See, for example, Thale, 117–18; Hardy (1959), 52.
6 'Man is part of Nature, and Nature is a vast and complex system of which the parts are subordinate to impersonal forces governing the whole.' Holloway, 124; see also Arnold Kettle, 'Middlemarch' in Swinden, 155.
7 Thale, 118.
8 James Sully (1881), 'George Eliot's Art', *Mind*, 6, 384–5.
9 'Idea and Image in the Novels of George Eliot' in Hardy (1970), 195–6.
10 After Mary Garth's effectual rejection of Mr Farebrother, 'it was impossible to help fleeting visions of another kind – new dignities and an acknowledged value of which she had often felt the absence' (570). See also Hardy (1959), 143–8.
11 David Carroll (1959), 'Unity Through Analogy: An Interpretation of *Middlemarch*' in *Victorian Studies*, II, 313.
12 See W. J. Harvey, 'The Intellectual Background of the Novel: Casaubon and Lydgate' in Hardy (1967) 34–6.

13 Mintz, 77. See also Harvey, note 16 above.
14 See Chapter 4 below.
15 See Harvey (1962), Davis (2006) 38–9 for fuller discussion of these issues in relation to this passage.
16 See below, p. 69 where narrator asserts the necessity of belief.
17 See Chapter 4 below, pp. 109–12.
18 See Chapter 4 below, p. 103.
19 James in Gard (ed.), 77; Leavis, 75; McSweeney, 84.
20 See Beaty (1961) for a discussion of the relevant changes.
21 See George Levine, 'The Hero as Dilettante: *Middlemarch* and *Nostromo*' in Smith (ed.), 162.
22 Thale, 113.
23 'Dorothea and the Theresa-Complex' in Swinden, 246.
24 Barbara Hardy, 'The Moment of Disenchantment' in Creeger, 61–2.

STUDY QUESTIONS

1 'It is the habit of my imagination to strive after as full a vision of the medium in which a character moves as of the character itself.' In what varied ways does the novel seeks to establish or suggest the community of *Middlemarch* in the following chapters/passages: 1 (pp. 7–11), 6, 8, 10 (pp. 86–92), 18, 45?

2 Consider the following critical dialogue about the issue of vocation in *Middlemarch*:

> Ironically, the character who stands firmly at the symbolic centre of the novel has no profession whatever. As a woman, Dorothea is not allowed direct access to the world possible for men . . . Dorothea's womanhood, instead of being an anomaly, is simply the most extreme example of the variety of constraints and contingencies that frustrate the urge to alter the world. The intensity of her desire and impossibility of her situation make Dorothea a kind of symbolic origin in relation to which the crowded cast of *Middlemarch* locate themselves. (Mintz, 60–1)

'The problem with this analysis', says Barrett, 'is that it turns Dorothea into a symbol that illuminates the vocational troubles of the men in the novel':

> It sees the vocational troubles of men as the central issue which Dorothea, as symbol, can illuminate. The reverse is the most likely and interesting possibility: because Dorothea's problem is the absence of vocation, that negative space must be defined, investigated, understood by reference to the positive forms that surround it . . . Dorothea's story is the investigation of an unrealised possibility . . . All the questions of vocation in the novel . . . reflect back upon the unavailable possibilities of Dorothea's vocational yearning. (Barrett, 131–2)

Are these positions as incompatible as they appear in this novel, which deals in mutually illuminating or reciprocally significant 'reversals' of perspective? 'What George Eliot claims for women in *Middlemarch* is not difference from men and not identity with them, but likeness to them in terms of capacity, predicament and endurance.' How far do you agree?

3 'Despite the central marital failures, the ideal of cooperative partnership is valued in this novel both as a possibility nurtured by the past, in the relationship of Fred and Mary, and as the hope of the future, in the relationship of Dorothea and Will. These relationships provide a counter-model to those of Dorothea and Casaubon, Lydgate and Rosamond.'

Examine, in the light of this possibility: Mary's rejection of Mr Farebrother in Chapter 52, and her statement to her father of her commitment to Fred in Chapter 86; and Dorothea's 'interviews' (as George Eliot called them) with Will in Chapters 22, 39, 37, 39, 54, 62, 83. Do you agree with Barbara Hardy that sensibility (unrealistically) replaces sensuality in their relationship? Or do you agree with Gillian Beer that what is said is less important in this relationship than the fact that something always *is* said, constantly, ceaselessly, without the lonely sundering silences which characterize the marital dialogues of the novel dialogues; and that their dialogues record 'the extent to which falling in love *is* conversation; the passionate discovery and exchange of meanings . . . [Dorothea's] attraction to Will grows through the play of spirit and learning between them: they teach each other. He frees her from desiring martyrdom; she gives him a great project.' (Beer, 1986: 174).

4 Trace the various types of reform (personal as well as public) which are tried, considered, enacted or recorded within the course of the novel. How successful do they prove to be? How do they contribute, if at all, to the novel's overall position on progress?

5 Consider, in the light of the discussions of religion in the novel in this chapter and in Chapter 1, the conversation between Will and Dorothea about personal belief in Chapter 39. 'Please not to call it by any name', says Dorothea. 'It is my life. I have found it out and cannot part with it. I have always been finding out my religion since I was a little girl.' Would it be fair to say that the personal and human content of belief is more important for George Eliot in *Middlemarch* than any name one might give it?

CHAPTER 4

CRITICAL RECEPTION AND PUBLISHING HISTORY

'No former book of mine has been received with more enthusiasm', George Eliot wrote after the publication of *Middlemarch* had been completed (*Journals* [1998], 142). Initially published in eight books between December 1871 and December 1872, by William Blackwood and Sons, the first four-volume edition was published simultaneously with Book VIII in December 1871, and re-issued in March 1873. The popularity of the novel is clear from the success of the one-volume Cheap edition which, published in May 1874, had sold 10,000 copies by the end of the year. The three-volume Cabinet edition, published in 1878, was the final main edition to appear in George Eliot's lifetime.

CONTEMPORARY RECEPTION

The many reviews of the novel were generally enthusiastic, and admiration was strong indeed from certain critics and reviewers. Edith Simcox, later a close friend and personal champion of George Eliot, wrote that *Middlemarch* 'marks an epoch in the history of fiction in so far as its incidents are taken from the inner life':

> The action is developed by the direct action of mind on mind and character on character, as the material circumstances of the outer world are made subordinate and accessory to the artistic presentation of a definite passage of mental experience, but chiefly as giving a background of perfect realistic truth to a profoundly imaginative psychological study. (*Critical Heritage*, 323)

George Eliot's powers as a psychological novelist also received exalted praise from one of her shrewdest and most prolific early reviewers, R. H. Hutton. In his review of Book Six, comparing her work to that of her popular contemporary, Anthony Trollope, he said:

> Mr Trollope scours a still greater surface of modern life with at least equal fidelity; but then how much less is the depth of drawing behind his figures! . . . He gives you where it is necessary the emotions proper to the situations, but rarely or never the emotions which lie concealed behind the situations and which give a kind of irony to them. His characters are carved out of the materials of ordinary society; George Eliot's include many which make ordinary society seem a sort of satire on the life behind. (*Critical Heritage*, 302)

One of the most famous and (still) influential contemporary reviews of *Middlemarch* came from Henry James: 'If we write novels so, how shall we write history?' he asked. As well as admiring the panoramic richness of the novel, James was effusive in his praise for what he called 'the superior quality of George Eliot's imagination', most especially evident, he felt, in her creation of character:

> Perception charged with feeling has constantly guided the author's hand, and yet her strokes remain as firm, her curves as free, her whole manner as serenely impersonal, as if, on a small scale, she were emulating the creative wisdom itself.

James's strongest reservation about the novel concerned its overall organization: 'That supreme sense of the vastness and variety of human life, under aspects apparently similar, which it belongs only to the greatest novels to produce' nonetheless resulted in a diffuseness of structure.[1] James also anticipated what was to become a common criticism of George Eliot's later work when he said: 'Many of the discursive passages of *Middlemarch* are, as we may say, too clever by half. The author wishes to say too many things and to say them too well.' Yet, at the same time, James felt that the 'intelligence' of George Eliot's imagination was one of the hallmarks of her greatness as a novelist:

> The constant presence of thought, of generalizing instinct, of *brain*, in a word, behind her observation, gives the latter its great

value and her whole manner its high superiority. It denotes a mind in which imagination is illumined by faculties rarely found in fellowship with it. (*Critical Muse*, 84)

Amid the general admiration for the novel, however, there were dissenting voices, even from those readers who had previously shown most appreciation of George Eliot's work. R. H. Hutton regretted both the emphasis on failure and disillusion and the absence – even positive rejection – of any spiritual or religious consolation in the novel:

> The whole tone of the story is so thoroughly noble, both morally and intellectually, that the care with which George Eliot excludes all real faith in God from the religious side of her characters, conveys the same sort of shock with which, during the early days of eclipses, men must have seen the rays of light converging towards a centre of darkness.

George Eliot, he said, 'is a melancholy teacher – melancholy because sceptical; and her melancholy scepticism is too apt to degenerate into scorn' (*Critical Heritage*, 313). Hutton's emphasis upon the 'melancholy' vision of *Middlemarch* echoes the complaint of a number of contemporary critics. Even Sydney Colvin's sensitively enthusiastic review of the novel draws attention to its note of deep 'sadness' and wonders how finally 'satisfying' such a work can be:

> Is it that a literature, which confronts all the problems of life and the world, and recognises all the springs of action, and all that clogs the springs, and all that comes from their smooth or impeded working, and all the importance of one life for the mass, – is it that such a literature must be like life itself, to leave us sad and hungry? (ibid., 338)

Hutton and Colvin were also among a number of reviewers who queried the novel's presentation of the relationship between individual and society, particularly where Dorothea was concerned. R. H. Hutton complained that the emphasis of the (original) penultimate paragraph of the novel (which blamed society for Dorothea's mistakes) 'had no foundation at all in the tale itself' (ibid., 307); and it is his objections which seem to have persuaded George Eliot to revise this paragraph of the Finale for later editions.[2]

DEATH AND DECLINE

With the publication of *Middlemarch*, George Eliot's reputation and prestige as a novelist reached its height. At the time of her death in 1880 she was generally regarded as the foremost English novelist. In the immediate aftermath of her death, Leslie Stephen, in his obituary article, began the trend of elevating the earlier works at the expense of the later ones that was to continue for the next half century and more. Her early novels, he wrote, 'have the unmistakable marks of high genius', while *Middlemarch*, 'though undoubtedly a powerful book', is 'to many readers a rather painful book . . . The light of day has most unmistakably superseded the indescribable glow which illuminated the earlier writings . . . [and] one cannot help regretting the loss of that earlier charm' (*Critical Heritage*, 469, 479). The novelist Anthony Trollope wrote in his autobiography (published in 1883) that 'in studying [George Eliot's] latter writings, one feels oneself to be in company with some philosopher rather than with a novelist' (Haight [1965], 150).

This emphasis upon the author's tendency towards the 'analytical' and philosophical is echoed in Henry James's general appraisal of the novelist's work in 1885. 'We feel in her always,' he wrote, 'that she proceeds from the abstract to the concrete, that her figures and situations are evolved . . . from her moral consciousness and are only indirectly the products of observation.' The novel for her, he said, 'was not primarily a picture of life . . . but a moralised fable, the last word of a philosophy trying to teach by example' (*Critical Heritage*, 497–8). James's criticisms were made in his review of the official biography of the author, *George Eliot's Life as Related in her Letters and Journals*, 'arranged and edited' by George Eliot's second husband, John Walter Cross, and published in 1885. Though still of immense importance to scholars and readers of George Eliot, Cross's work nonetheless contributed to the downturn in her critical reputation in the decades immediately following her death. His concern posthumously to confer upon the author the kind of moral respectability she had risked sacrificing in life (as a result of her relationship with George Henry Lewes) led Cross to produce what has come to be regarded as a selective and distortingly idealized picture of George Eliot as a rather dull, sententious moralist. This portrait of the novelist helped (but only helped) to make George Eliot a central target in the backlash against high Victorian culture that occurred among writers and critics in the 1890s and early twentieth century.

Writers as diverse as Samuel Butler, W. B. Yeats and George Bernard Shaw saw little to admire in George Eliot's work, finding it excessively moralistic, analytical or generally dispiriting. Her standing among critics fared little better. George Saintsbury reflected the general critical mood when, writing in 1895, he said, 'I never remember having read a single book of George Eliot's with genuine and whole-hearted admiration'. He described *Middlemarch* as an 'elaborate [study] . . . of immense effort and erudition not unenlightened by humour but on the whole dead' (Haight, 166–7).

W. C. Brownell, seeking, in 1901, to explain the then current reaction against George Eliot's work, pointed to the novelist's 'specifically intellectual interest' in her characters: 'our attention is so concentrated on what they think', he said, 'that we hardly know how they feel, or whether . . . they feel at all . . . The soul, the temperament, the heart . . . the whole nature plays a subordinate part'. Brownell adds that this 'intellectual preoccupation' with 'mental perplexities' is 'fatal to action': 'in George Eliot's world nothing ever happens' (ibid., 171). Leslie Stephen's important and judicious full-length study of George Eliot, published in 1902, also regretted what he called 'the philosophical detachment' which 'exhibits her characters in a rather distorting light'. It is for this reason, he says, that *Middlemarch*, for all its 'extraordinary power' and 'subtle and accurate observation', seems to fall short of the great masterpieces, which imply a closer contact with the world of realities and 'less preoccupation with certain speculative doctrines'.[3] Oliver Elton, writing in 1920, likewise complained of George Eliot that 'while exhaustively describing life she is likely to miss the spirit of life itself'. He describes *Middlemarch* as 'almost one of the great novels of the language' but wishes for 'a little more ease and play and simplicity, a little less of the anxious idealism which ends in going beyond nature' (Haight, 192).

The first important (albeit qualified) challenge to the 'late Victorian version' of George Eliot came in Virginia Woolf's centenary tribute of 1919. In this portrait the moralizing sage is transformed into a woman of 'astonishing intellectual vitality', whose immense creative energy was liberated when she found personal happiness and love in her relationship with George Henry Lewes. Moreover, Woolf praised rather than deplored the 'searching power

and reflective richness' of the later works, and reversed the trend of
relegating the latter in favour of the early novels when she wrote
(now famously): 'It is not that her power diminished, for, to our
thinking, it is at its highest in the mature *Middlemarch*, the
magnificent book which with all its imperfections is one of the few
English novels written for grown-up people' (ibid., 184–7). Yet
Woolf's tribute did not significantly improve George Eliot's critical
reputation. In 1934, Lord David Cecil accounted for what he called
'the catastrophic slump' in her popularity by the 'exclusively moral
point of view' which leads the novelist to confront human nature 'a
little like a school-teacher; kindly but just, calm but censorious,
with birch-rod in hand to use as she thinks right'. Describing
Middlemarch as George Eliot's 'masterpiece', and applauding its
Tolstoyan largeness of subject, Cecil nonetheless criticized the limitation of her range – '*Middlemarch* may be the nearest English
equivalent to *War and Peace, but* it is a provincial sort of *War and
Peace*' – as well as her inability to 'give us that intense unalloyed
pleasure we get from the greatest masters' (ibid., 207–10).

REVALUATION

It was not until the years immediately following the Second World
War that interest was revived in George Eliot's work by a new generation of critics, who were part of a renewed wave of interest in the
Victorian period as a whole. 'Probably no English writer of the time',
Basil Willey wrote in 1949, 'and certainly no novelist, more fully
epitomises the century' (ibid., 260). In 1946, V. S. Pritchett showed
the appreciation for her mature work which it had enjoyed in the
writer's own lifetime: 'No Victorian novel', he said, 'approaches
Middlemarch in its width of reference, its intellectual power, or the
imperturbable spaciousness of its narrative' (ibid., 210). The work
which most decisively turned the tide of George Eliot's critical fortunes in the immediate post-war period was F. R. Leavis's *The Great
Tradition*, published in 1948. Leavis situated George Eliot among
the 'great' novelists of English literature – along with Jane Austen,
Henry James, Joseph Conrad and D. H. Lawrence – and singled out
Middlemarch as the novel which demonstrated most fully those qualities which characterized George Eliot's 'genius': her moral seriousness, her profound intellect (allied with an 'emotional quality'), and
her incomparably searching psychological analysis. Leavis is highly

critical, however, of the book's major weakness as he sees it – the author's 'unqualified self-identification' with her heroine, Dorothea, whom Leavis regarded as 'a day-dream ideal self' onto whom George Eliot self-indulgently projected adolescently immature longings of her own.[4]

The critical preoccupation with George Eliot's work, and the rehabilitation of her reputation, was given a further boost with the publication in 1954–5 of seven volumes of Gordon S. Haight's edition of *The George Eliot Letters*, which made available substantial new information about the author.[5] Within several years came two of the most influential full-length studies of George Eliot's work. Barbara Hardy's *The Novels of George Eliot: A Study in Form*, (1959) and W. J. Harvey's *The Art of George Eliot* (1961) set out to demonstrate that George Eliot was a 'great formal artist', in conscious rebuttal of the Jamesian view of the author's 'indifference' to form. 'George Eliot's composition', Hardy said, 'is usually as complex and as subtle as the composition of Henry James or Proust or Joyce, but it is very much less conspicuous because of the engrossing realistic interest of her human and social delineation' (Hardy [1959], 5). Harvey's complementary study related the author's formal method to the moral-philosophical thinking that informs her novels, arguing that George Eliot's formal art is complexly 'subtle and flexible' in implicit recognition that 'life is rarely a matter of simple categories' (Harvey, 55). This period also saw a growing interest in George Eliot's intellectual development, with the publication in 1965 of Bernard Paris's *Experiments in Life: George Eliot's Quest for Values*, which offered the first full-length study of the intellectual ideas and influences that had helped to shape her thinking and the moral pattern of her novels, and of U. C. Knoepflmacher's *Religious Humanism and the Victorian Novel*, which explored George Eliot's scientific positivism and her Feuerbachian 'humanization' of Christianity.

Some of the critics cited above are represented in Barbara Hardy's important collection of essays on *Middlemarch: Critical Approaches to the Novel* (1967). In her introduction to that collection, Hardy says: 'if a poll were held for the greatest English novel there would probably be more votes for *Middlemarch* than for any other work.' This observation is a measure of how far George Eliot's reputation had recovered from the slump it suffered in the immediate post-Victorian era. It is arguable, however, that with Hardy's tribute we reach the zenith of George Eliot's critical acclaim in the twentieth century.

RECENT AND CURRENT DEVELOPMENTS

One shorthand way of charting the interpretation of *Middlemarch* over the past half century is to survey the critical and theoretical readings of the novel's image of the web. For W. J. Harvey writing in the 1960s, the web was expressive of George Eliot's 'imperative . . . "only connect"'. It signified 'not just her deepest sense of what life in all its complications is like, but also her awareness of the novelist's duty to give form and significance to the flux and chaos of existence' (Harvey, 241). For Harvey the web was a 'key' to the novel's formal and philosophical unity. For Mark Schorer, too, the 'metaphorical system' of the novel and the ways in which characters 'share' in it demonstrated the thorough 'integration' of George Eliot's mind and literary operation, and overcame the 'technical paradox' this novel presents as a work of 'widely diffused story materials' with a nonetheless 'powerful effect of unity'.[6] Both critics were writing in conscious opposition to the inherited Jamesian objection to the novel's large, loose bagginess.

Marxist Readings
Arnold Kettle's earlier Marxist study of *Middlemarch*, however, had argued that the novel's vision of 'the stealthy convergence of human lots' figures the author's conception of society as a mechanistic, determining force. She understands society's power but not its dynamism, he said, so that her social vision remains 'static' and even at odds with the novel's emphasis upon the power of individual moral choices.[7] Terry Eagleton's later (and still most influential) Marxist reading interprets such counter-currents ideologically. For Eagleton the web imagery is George Eliot's means of imposing a 'falsifying' formal unity upon elements within the novel which are ideologically in conflict with one another. The novel is deeply committed, argued Eagleton, on the one hand, to 'Romantic individualism, concerned with the untrammelled evolution of the "free spirit"' and, on the other, to 'certain "higher" corporate ideological modes' (such as Feuerbachian humanism), which 'seek to identify the immutable social laws' that place all individuals within 'a totalising collective'. Eliot's project, said Eagleton, is to resolve the

contradiction between a belief in social totality and collectivism on the one hand and the drive for personal self-fulfilment on the other. The project fails, he said, because what the novel demonstrates in the stories of its protagonists is not only 'the bleak victory of an entrenched provincial consciousness over . . . Romantic drives to transcend it' but the failure of totalizing projects themselves. Each of the four major characters represents an ideological total-ization that is typical of the age: 'Casaubon idealism, Lydgate scientific rationalism, Bulstrode Evangelical Christianity, Dorothea Romantic self-achievement through a unifying principle of action. Each of these totalities crumbles, ensnared in the quotidian':

> The web's complex fragility impels a prudent political conser-vatism: the more delicately interlaced its strands, the more dis-ruptive consequences of action can multiply, and so the more circumspect one must be in launching ambitiously totalising pro-jects. Yet, conversely, if action at any point in the web will vibrate through its filaments to affect the whole formation, a semi-mystical relationship to the totality is nevertheless preserved. Here . . . imagery is exploited to signify how a fulfilling relation to the social totality can be achieved, not by ideological abstrac-tion, but by pragmatic, apparently peripheral work . . . The problem of totality within the novel is effectively displaced to the question of aesthetic form itself . . . The novel, in other words, formally answers the problem it thematically poses.

One of the major ironies of the novel for Eagleton is that while the ensnarement of each ideological totality shows George Eliot's deep suspicion of the same, and offers 'a salutary empiricist check to the tyranny of theoreticism', the author's will to reconcile historical con-tradictions between the needs of self and of society results in a novel which is a 'triumph of aesthetic totalisation'.[8]

Post-structural and Deconstructive Readings
By the 1970s, studies of George Eliot's work had inevitably begun to be influenced by the new currents in English literary criticism, and particularly the new theoretical approaches developed on the continent. The structuralist concern with language, and the ways in which the latter 'constructs' reality in accordance with a society's governing ideology, gave rise to a number of trenchant critiques of

nineteenth-century realism and its claims to be a window onto the world that faithfully represents reality. One of the most significant of these critiques came from Colin MacCabe (1979), for whom *Middlemarch* was a 'classic realist text' (the term is pejorative in MacCabe's usage) insofar as it purports to represent an unproblematic reality while in fact offering a highly selective account or version of the same. The novel, MacCabe argues, creates a hierarchy of discourses, in which the narrative voice dominates, interpreting and controlling the other discourses and claiming privileged access to a final, single, knowable truth or reality. This apparently self-evident reality, moreover, accords with and repeats the received forms of reality transmitted by a society's ideological and cultural codes.[9]

J. Hillis Miller is one of the most important deconstructive critics of George Eliot. He also views *Middlemarch* as an ideologically motivated construction of reality, and reads its imagery in the light of the novelist's 'enterprise of totalisation'; but, rather differently to Eagleton and MacCabe, Miller argues that the novel 'elaborately deconstructs' or undermines the ideological assumptions upon which it rests. The 'all-encompassing' metaphor of the web presents a 'single, comprehensive model or picture of Middlemarch society as being a complex moving medium, tightly interwoven into a single fabric', and works as an 'interpretative net' or 'paradigm by means of which to think of the whole'. By implication the medium in question can be scientifically observed and objectively and finally understood. Yet these 'apparently clear-cut, objectivist implications' of the metaphor of the web, says Hillis Miller, are crossed, contaminated and undercut by the prevalent 'metaphor of vision' within the novel, which reportedly – and most emphatically in the image of the pier-glass which opens Chapter 27 – suggests that each individual sees his or her own (subjectivist) totality. One is forced to deduce from this pattern of imagery, says Hillis Miller, that 'Middlemarch society perhaps appears to be a web only because a certain kind of subjective light [the author-narrator's] is concentrated on it'. He concludes:

> [The metaphorical models in *Middlemarch*] are multiple and incompatible . . . This incoherent, heterogeneous, 'unreadable', or nonsynthesisable quality of the text . . . jeopardises the narrator's effort of totalisation. It suggests that one gets a different kind of totality depending on what metaphorical model is used.

The presence of several incompatible models brings into the open the arbitrary and partial character of each and so ruins the claim of the narrator to have a total, unified and impartial vision. What is true for the characters of *Middlemarch*, 'that we all of us, grave or light, get our thoughts entangled in metaphors, and act fatally on the strength of them' must also be true for the narrator. The web of interpretative figures cast by the narrator over the characters becomes a net in which the narrator himself [sic] is entangled and trapped, his sovereign vision blinded.[10]

Feminist Criticism

Alongside readings that proved to be classics not only of *Middlemarch* criticism but in their respective theoretical fields, feminist criticism was also concerned with the extent to which George Eliot's work transmits or critiques prevailing ideologies, but had a more specific interest in how far the author seems to have accepted or rejected the patriarchal values of her time. The early feminist criticism of the 1970s was largely hostile to George Eliot, focusing on her conservative portrayal of women as embodying the traditional virtues of submission and renunciation. As Kate Millet put it in *Sexual Politics* (1970): 'Dorothea's predicament in *Middlemarch* is an eloquent plea that a fine mind be allowed an occupation; but it goes no further than petition. She married Will Ladislaw and can expect no more of life than the discovery of a good companion whom she can serve as a secretary' (Millett, 139). Even Ellen Moers who, in her *Literary Women* (1978), helps to place George Eliot within a tradition of women's writing, attacks the novelist roundly for being 'no feminist': 'George Eliot was always concerned with the superior, large-souled woman whose distinction lies not in her deeds but in her capacity to attract attention and arouse admiration . . . [Dorothea Brooke] is good for nothing but to be admired. An arrogant, selfish, spoiled, rich beauty, she does but little harm in the novel' (194).

Such views were both surveyed and critiqued by Zelda Austen and by Elaine Showalter,[11] whose ground-breaking *A Literature of Their Own* situated George Eliot squarely among contemporary nineteenth-century women writers, tracing her influence upon, and kinship with them.[12] One of the most influential feminist studies was that of Sandra Gilbert and Susan Gubar. Starting from a central thesis that nineteenth-century women writers were covertly reacting not only to their confinement as women in a patriarchal world, but to their confinement as writers within a male literary tradition and male literary forms, they found in George Eliot's work a suppressed feminine rage at the restrictions upon a woman's power to write: they read *Middlemarch* as fundamentally concerned with 'the potential for violence in the two conflicting sides of [George Eliot] that she identifies as the masculine mind and the feminine heart . . . The novel is centrally concerned with the tragic complicity and resulting violence of men and women inhabiting a culture defined as masculine' (Gilbert and Gubar, 500). The most scholarly, historical and imaginatively literary feminist study of the author is that of Gillian Beer. Her interpretation of the novel's imagery as formally supporting the novel's *in toto* proposition that 'the proper and liberating task [is] that of making connections, not seeking origins' also implicitly challenges some of the 'totalizing' readings discussed above:

> We are not, as readers, obliged to carry the burden of [the] characters' disappointment without relief. We have access to a world compacted of meaning, yet so profuse that we need not even expect to raise all connections into consciousness. This quality of explanation means that the exhaustiveness of explanation does not enclose or imprison text and reader. Explanation is preceded and surpassed by the condensed form of image, and the sources of that imagery range wide across human knowledge . . . The activity of the text, through imagery and imagination, makes us join in understanding that the 'ordinary' is freighted with fullest potential. (Beer [1986], 192–4, 199)

George Eliot and Science

Beer's thesis builds on her study of the dynamic interrelationship between evolutionary theory and narrative practice in *Middlemarch*, in *Darwin's Plots: Evolutionary Narrative in Darwin, George Eliot and Nineteenth-Century Fiction* (1983), now a standard work of this critical genre. Beer demonstrates that the scientific allusions and parallels in the novel are not merely intellectual elaboration but testimony to the novel's committed engagement with contemporary scientific enquiry, such that 'Darwin's insights and the difficulties raised by those insights move into the substance of the [novel's] projects'. Relating the novel's concern with 'relations', in particular its metaphor of the web, to the 'inextricable web of affinities' proposed by Darwin's *Origin of Species*, Beer concluded that 'diversification, not truth to type, is the creative principle' of George Eliot's later fiction, as it is the cornerstone of Darwinian theory.[13] A second classic in this field, Sally Shuttleworth's *George Eliot and Nineteenth-Century Science: The Make-Believe of a Beginning* (1984), focuses upon organic theory, and the attraction it held for George Eliot in emphasizing the interdependence of part and whole, and in offering a scientific basis for ethical conduct. While this organicist philosophy found relatively unproblematic expression in the earlier novels, in *Middlemarch*, with its continual shifts in perspective (reflecting the complexly mixed nature of the social organism), George Eliot reveals, it is argued, a recognition of the disjunction between a scientific moral ideal and social reality.

Current Developments

For recent important work on George Eliot and Victorian science of mind and the developing discipline of psychology, see Rick Rylance, (2000) *Victorian Psychology and British Culture 1850–1880* and Michael Davis (2006) *George Eliot and Nineteenth-Century Psychology: Exploring the Unmapped Country*. George Eliot's relationship with non-literary artistic disciplines has been explored in two original and scholarly works, Hugh Witemeyer (1979), *George Eliot and the Visual Arts* and Beryl Gray (1989), *George Eliot and Music*, and more recently in Delia Da Sousa Correa (2002), *George Eliot, Music and Victorian Culture*. Judith Johnston (2006), *George Eliot and the Discourses of Medievalism* explores George Eliot's use of motifs of chivalric romance and allegory in *Middlemarch*, building on the earlier work of Barry Qualls (1981), *The Secular Pilgrim of Victorian Fiction*, which interpreted *Middlemarch* as the creation of a new mythology based on Bunyan's *Pilgrim's Progress*. Other important work has considered George Eliot in relation to close contemporary English influences on the one hand – see Nancy L. Paxton, *George Eliot and Herbert Spencer: Feminism, Evolutionism and the Reconstruction of Gender* – and to the European heritage on the other: see John Rignall (ed.) (1997), *George Eliot and Europe*.

NOTES

1 See above, Chapter 2, pp. 31–48.
2 See above, Chapter 3, p. 75.

3 Leslie Stephen (1902), *George Eliot*. London: Macmillan, 184.
4 See Chapter 3 above, p. 87.
5 Haight's painstaking scholarship culminated in the publication of his biography of George Eliot in 1968, which replaced Cross's as the definitive version of her life.
6 Mark Schorer, 'The Structure of the Novel: Method, Metaphor and Mind' in Hardy (1967), 12, 22.
7 'Middlemarch' in Swinden, 155–6.
8 'George Eliot, Ideology and Literary Form' (1976) in Peck, 33, 37–8. For a contrasting reading of the significance of the weblike inter-relatedness of social action in the novel see George Levine (1962), 'Determinism and Responsibility' in Haight, 349–60.
9 Colin MacCabe (1978), 'The End of a Metalanguage: From George Eliot to *Dubliners*' in Newton, 156–66.
10 'Optic and Semiotic in Middlemarch' in Peck, 80.
11 In their articles 'Why Feminist Critics Are Angry With George Eliot' (1976) in *College English*, 37, 6, 549–61 and 'The Greening of Sister George' (1980) in *Nineteenth-Century Fiction*, 35, 3, 292–311.
12 See Showalter, Chapter IV, 100–52.
13 See Beer (1983), 167–80.

STUDY QUESTIONS

1 Terence Wright has argued that 'no single reading can hope to be "complete", as if reproducing a tapestry by following a design'. Readings, he says, which interpret the novel in terms of its spatial metaphor (the web) 'falsify the process of reading, neglecting both its temporal dimension [the fact that we read the novel forward in time] and its context (which will always change)' so that any critical reading will be subject to the historical-cultural conditions in which it is operating. Like Gillian Beer, he concludes: 'The very richness of metaphor in *Middlemarch* . . . preserves an element of play, allowing a certain freedom of interpretation' (Wright, 38). How useful do you find this comment as a 'key' to negotiating the multiplicity of critical approaches the novel has generated?

2 Test the theses of three critics selected here (Schorer, Hillis Miller and Davis, for example, or Schorer, Eagleton and Beer) in relation to specific, 'live' examples of the use of the web or related imagery in the novel: see, for instance 22, 58, 93–4, 115–16, 125, 128, 139, 143, 146, 178, 297, 342, 487, 656. Do these readings seem historically successive and thus mutually cancelling/incompatible, or are they mutually illuminating?

CHAPTER 5

ADAPTATION, INTERPRETATION AND INFLUENCE

ADAPTATION

The rich interpretative afterlife of *Middlemarch* might have been a disappointment to George Eliot, one feels, since it has not been consistently matched by the novel's influence in the world beyond that of academic criticism. One great boost to the novel's popularity came with Andrew Davies's BBC drama adaptation in 1994. This was the second adaptation of the novel for the BBC. While the first, directed by Joan Craft in 1968, had proved unsuccessful, Davies's adaptation was a popular triumph, and sent the Penguin paperback edition of the novel to the top of the bestseller's list. It was universally acclaimed for its quality as television – a classic in a long tradition of impeccably made BBC 'classic serials'; but as an 'edition' of the novel, it had its detractors: 'Lavishly costumed, expensively authenticated', the adaptation's concern was 'not so much to understand [the] book . . . as to find an exact equivalent for as much of it as possible', such that 'its authenticity is the most inauthentic thing about it' (Gervais, 59). It was also criticized for exploiting those elements of the novel that lent themselves most readily to screen-adaptation – its stories of young love, of blackmail, of suspicion of murder, as well as its original serialization in bi-monthly and monthly parts – and in the process sacrificing 'complexity . . . for costume' and reducing 'scope . . . to soap' (O'Keeffe, 7–8).

Much of this reductionist soaping has to do with the difficulty of translating the prose that gives *Middlemarch* its identity to a televisual medium. For example, the opening sequence of the adaptation shows Lydgate arriving in a Middlemarch bustling with the activity of market-trade and business, and in the midst of which the railway is being built: 'The future', says Lydgate. While the visual-thematic connection thus enforced between Lydgate and the forces of modernity is sanctioned by the operation of the novel (see p. 11 above), the emphasis upon it at the outset forgoes the pervasiveness of the effect wrought by the opening of George Eliot's *Middlemarch* – the one and a half page Prelude. 'This is a serious omission', claim McKillop and Platt:

> The Prelude guides our subsequent reading, setting the grave, solemn tone which ensures that we do not feel somehow cheated by the final fate of the leading characters. The sense of wastage at the end of the novel does not take the reader by surprise. Without the Prelude (or any sense of it) . . . the ending is in danger of seeming an unprepared anti-climax. The novel's . . . meaning is built on the foundation of knowledge: this is what gives the novel its tragic dimension, its 'Greekness'. In the serial, as in many unnarrated fictions, knowledge is successively and therefore temptingly revealed to the reader. Gravity is replaced by suspense. In the serial we suspect something will become of Lydgate; in the novel we *know* it, and build on this knowledge.

A further significant departure of this 'unnarrated fiction' for these critics is that the 'intimate style does not dominate':

> *Middlemarch* . . . is an anti-visual novel . . . Significant visual detail in Eliot often takes the form of internalised imagery within a character's thought process. 'Language gives a fuller image, which is all the better for being vague,' wrote Eliot. 'The true seeing is within, and painting stares at you with an insistent perfection.'

Some of the adaptation's attempts to recover George Eliot's inner voice seem rather clumsily to misfire. Even the gravity of Dame Judi Dench's final voice-over rounding up characters' fates, for instance, cannot dispel a sense of anti-climax tempered neither by the sad sense of irony, nor by the prizing of the hidden, diffuse effects of the anonymous, unhistoric life which characterizes the Finale of the novel. Moreover, the occasional shifting of original narratorial comments to pronouncements of character – a version of 'the roar on the other side of silence' commentary is given, late in the serial, to

Juliet Aubrey's (excellent) Dorothea, for example – only highlights the degree to which George Eliot's language seems to exceed the capacity of an ordinary human to embody it. It is because such recognitions and their articulation are not readily available even to the moral earnestness of a Dorothea (in whom their expression jars incongruously and faintly comically in the adaptation) that *Middlemarch* came to be written.

For Lothe, however, the adaptation also exploits its medium in ways which not only satisfactorily retain but also accentuate the meanings of the narrator's discourse. A scene in the Vatican when Dorothea and Casaubon are on honeymoon 'presents a medium shot of Casaubon bent over his books, working in the silence of the library and yet hearing Dorothea's voice saying to him "Isn't it time to begin . . . to make your vast knowledge known to the world?" ':

> Because her voice is audible as voice-over only, it acquires a narrative authority comparable to that of the novel's third-person narrator. Suddenly we understand that Casaubon will never publish his 'Key to All Mythologies' and we also gather that Dorothea's suspicion that he may be unable to do so is actually shared by Casaubon himself.

The 'deanthropomorphized' camera eye is also used to imitate or approximate to George Eliot's 'commitment to a form of narrative presentation that, although it neither can nor wishes to be "neutral" ' aims at once 'to understand the interests, desires and motivating forces of all the characters', while simultaneously exposing 'partial' ways of knowing a character – 'the narrator's account, the report of other characters, or the inward reflections of a self' – as misleading:

> The film camera can register the effect of seeing one character on another in a manner that makes visually accessible to the viewer a double image, that of the figure of 'the known' along with that of the figure of 'the knowing'. Such an effect is achieved [by] combining a series of medium and long shots [to present] the Casaubons' arrival at Lowick in a manner that highlights the contrast between husband and wife. Characteristically untactful, Mr Brooke comments that Mr Casaubon looks 'a little pale'. This is an obvious and yet interesting variant of seeing: though superficial in his dealing with others, Mr Brooke can still see,

more clearly than Dorothea, that Casaubon is ageing rapidly . . . [Such scenes] exploit film's capacity for showing faces, and facial expressions, in a way that prompts interpretive activity on the part of the viewer. (ibid., 193–4)

Thus the 'multifaceted' role of George Eliot's third-person narrator, 'who, although she can see what the characters fail to see, links her perspective to them in a sustained narrative act of human solidarity and compassion' (ibid., 197), is in part restored in the adaptation by extensive and skilful use of the 'mutiplexity' of filmic narrative.

Andrew Davies is currently writing the script for the first film adaptation of *Middlemarch*. A Hollywood collaboration, with Sam Mendes as director, the film is due for release in 2009 (casting is yet to be announced). The disproportion between the richness and expansiveness of the novel and the length and stricture of a big-screen format might seem as initially incongruous as the mismatch between George Eliot's nineteenth-century provincial England and the British director's hitherto exclusively, even fiercely American concerns. Yet Mendes' previous work (*American Beauty*, for example) has the kind of epic scope, vision and ambition a successful screen rendition of *Middlemarch* will certainly demand.

INFLUENCE

'What do I think of *Middlemarch*?' wrote Emily Dickinson in 1873. 'What do I think of glory – except that in a few instances this "mortal" has already put on immortality. George Eliot is one.' A sense of the inimitable grandeur of George Eliot's achievement had impressed fellow novelists in England, even those whose work had influenced George Eliot's own. Elizabeth Gaskell had felt it was 'not worthwhile trying to write while there are such books as George Eliot's', and Margaret Oliphant wrote ruefully in her *Authobiography*, 'No one even will mention me in the same breath as George Eliot. And that is just'. Yet the mature realist work of these writers owes much to her example, just as the success of Thomas Hardy's Darwinian provincialism and Henry James's penetrating psychological study of Isabel Archer in *The Portrait of a Lady* are unthinkable without the model of George Eliot's late fiction.

In the twentieth century, Virginia Woolf's enthusiastic admiration, against the modernist grain, for her predecessor's work gave

rise to intense feminist-critical focus on the artistic and philosophical affiliations between two authors who were so decisive in shaping
the contours of a female tradition of writing. *To the Lighthouse* pays
explicit (ironic) homage to *Middlemarch* when a character leaves the
third volume on the train. But the influence of the novel tacitly and
palpably lives in Woolf's abundantly flexible exploitation of free
indirect mode to register the simultaneity and connectedness, in
terms of pain, loss and need, of nonetheless strandedly individuated
and human lives, for whom the possibility of overcoming separateness exists only in glimpsed 'fragments'. While D. H. Lawrence and
Marcel Proust were avowed, even passionate admirers of George
Eliot's early work, it is the tradition she initiated in *Middlemarch* of
(said Lawrence) putting all the action on the inside that the work of
these writers honoured and continued.

On the whole, however, the self-conscious formalism of the modernist movement was inimical to the apparently unaesthetic moral
seriousness of George Eliot's mature work, a hostility deplored and
challenged by Iris Murdoch in the mid-twentieth century. She
found it 'unpardonable' that T. S. Eliot should have 'cast his vote
against George Eliot's work', which, for Murdoch, displayed an
almost Shakespearean capacity for 'so respecting and loving her
characters as to make them exist as free and separate beings'. The
twentieth-century novel, Murdoch said, was a degenerate descen-
dant of nineteenth-century literary realism: for the 'spread-out
substantial picture of the manifold virtues' of self and society, and
of individuals 'against a background of values, of realities, which
transcend [them]', the modern novel substituted 'a brave naked will
surrounded by an uneasily comprehended empirical world'. That
individual nakedness and incomprehension made the novel all the
more 'essential' as a response to a 'deep and ordinary human need'
– a claim for the importance of the novel which puts Murdoch
squarely in the tradition pioneered by George Eliot. Murdoch's
own most successful attempts at realism, says A. S. Byatt, present
a world 'delicately analysed with the combination of intellectual
grasp and sensuous immediacy of George Eliot'. The same might
be observed of Byatt's own work where the relation of ideas to
fiction which she admires in George Eliot's work finds a contemporary home. The most 'vital discovery' Byatt learned from reading
Middlemarch when she was starting out as a novelist 'was that her
people *think*': 'For many writers, and many readers, including

myself, the thought of "the novel" in the abstract is followed by the image of *Middlemarch* in the particular.' Traces of that generic haunting can be found even in the experimental (English) realism of, for instance, Graham Swift in *Waterland* (1983): 'For the reality of things – be thankful – only visits us for a brief while' bears witness to the paradox of literary realism – its power to disclose within imagined ordinariness what ordinary life mostly conceals – as if to reclaim for the twentieth century the significance of George Eliot's 'roar on the other side of silence'. But this is a reader's novel as much as a writer's, 'one of the few English novels written for grown-up people', said Virginia Woolf. One is a long time grown-up in that mid-life region where paths narrow or close as they do for the characters of *Middlemarch*. The free life of this novel, so much prized by Iris Murdoch, leaves room for continued growth even in its most grown-up readers.

STUDY QUESTIONS

1 Compare the novel's celebrated window scene in Chapter 80 (as well as its prelude and aftermath) with its rendition in one or more screen adaptations. Consider how technical effects (the use of flashback in the BBC 1994 version, for example) and artistic licence/interpretation (Dorothea leaves her window literally to become 'part' of the 'palpitating' life she sees outside of it in Davies's 1994 screenplay) help to preserve (or not) the quasi-religious power of the original. Are other sources of power unlocked? If so, how?

2 A. S. Byatt has said that as a novelist of ideas, George Eliot 'has no real heir . . . in England': 'she was European, not little English, her roots were Dante, Goethe, Shakespeare, Balzac.' Does this help to explain why *Middlemarch* tends not to fit easily into the categories to which it is customarily assigned (e.g. the Great English Tradition; women's writing; the historical novel)?

FURTHER READING

CHAPTER 1: CONTEXTS

Letters and Biography

Ashton, Rosemary (1996) *George Eliot: A Life*. Harmondsworth: Penguin Books Ltd.

Cross, J. W. (1885) *George Eliot's Life as Related in her Letters and Journals*. 3 vols. Edinburgh: Blackwood and Sons. (Selective but still important record of George Eliot's life from her notebooks and letters.)

Haight, Gordon S. (1954–78) *The George Eliot Letters*. 9 vols. New Haven and London: Yale University Press. (Indispensable resource for scholarship and criticism upon which all subsequent biographies have been based.)

Levine, George (ed.) (2001) *The Cambridge Companion to George Eliot*. Cambridge: Cambridge University Press.

Redinger, Ruby (1976) *George Eliot: The Emergent Self*. London: Bodley Head. (Sensitively interpretative account of George Eliot's inner life and her emergence as a novelist. Remains the best alternative to the more official versions of her life.)

Rignall, John (2000) *Oxford Reader's Companion to George Eliot*. Oxford: Oxford University Press.

See also:

Hardy, Barbara (2006) *George Eliot: A Critic's Biography*. London: Continuum.

Nestor, Pauline (2002) *George Eliot*. Basingstoke: Palgrave.

Early Writings

Ashton, Rosemary (1992) *George Eliot, Selected Critical Writings*. Oxford: Oxford University Press. (Contains most important essays and reviews, and extracts from translations of Strauss, Feuerbach and Spinoza.)

Byatt, A. S. (ed.) (1990) *George Eliot: Selected Essays, Poems and Other Writings*. Harmondsworth, Middlesex: Penguin Books Ltd. (Also contains important early writings and translations.)

Notebooks and Journals

Harris, Margaret and Johnston, Judith (eds) (1998) *The George Eliot Journals*. Cambridge: Cambridge University Press.

Pratt, John Clark and Neufeldt, Victor A. (eds) (1979) *George Eliot's 'Middlemarch' Notebooks: A Transcription*. Berkeley: University of California Press. (Contains George Eliot's notes of her literary and historical research from 1868 to 1871.)

The Victorian Novel and its Context

David, Deirdre (ed.) (2001) *The Cambridge Companion to the Victorian Novel*. Cambridge: Cambridge University Press.

Davis, Philip (2002) *The Victorians. The Oxford English Literary History*, 8. Oxford: Oxford University Press.

Gilmour, Robin (1986) *The Novel in the Victorian Age: A Modern Introduction*. London: Edward Arnold.

Wheeler, Michael (1994) *English Fiction of the Victorian Period 1830–1890*. 2nd edition. *Longman Literature in English*. London: Longman.

CHAPTER 2: LANGUAGE, STYLE, GENRE

Ashton, Rosemary (1983) *George Eliot*. Oxford: Oxford University Press. (Useful introduction, which outlines the influence of Comte, Feuerbach and Spinoza.)

Beaty, Jerome (1961) *'Middlemarch' from Notebook to Novel: A Study in George Eliot's Creative Method*. Urbana: University of Illinois Press.

Beer, Gillian (1986) *George Eliot. Key Women Writers*. Hemel Hempstead: Harvester Wheatsheaf. (Excellent critical study and the most scholarly feminist reading of the novels.)

Chase, Karen (ed.) (2006) *Middlemarch in the 21ˢᵗ Century*. Oxford: Oxford University Press. (New collection of essays by established critics – Beer, Chase, Flint, Deeds Ermarth, Hillis Miller among others – on *Middlemarch* as an 'open text' resistant to definitive readings: includes chapter on 1994 BBC TV adaptation.)

Ermarth, Elizabeth Deeds (1985) *George Eliot*. Boston: Twayne Publishers. (Also pays due regard to essays and translations.)

Hardy, Barbara (1959) *The Novels of George Eliot: A Study in Form*. London: Athlone Press. (Most influential early full-length study of George Eliot's work, and remains one of the best critical studies.)

Hardy, Barbara (1967) *Middlemarch: Critical Approaches to the Novel*. New York: Oxford University Press. (Important collection of essays, which includes: Mark Schorer, 'The Structure of the Novel'; W. J. Harvey, 'The Intellectual Background of the Novel'; Jerome Beaty, 'The Text of the Novel'; Derek Oldfield, 'The Language of the Novel'.)

Harvey, W. J. (1962) *The Art of George Eliot*. New York: Oxford University Press.

Knoepflmacher, U. C. (1965) *Religious Humanism and the Victorian Novel: George Eliot, Walter Pater and Samuel Butler*. Princeton, NJ: Princeton University Press. (Argues that George Eliot's intellectual beliefs should not be regarded separately from her art, but as integral to it, since they are transmuted into form in her novels.)

Miller, D. A. (1981) *Narrative and Its Discontents: Problems of Closure in the Traditional Novel*. Princeton, NJ: Princeton University Press. (Contains influential chapter on *Middlemarch*.)

Paris, Bernard (1965) *Experiments in Life: George Eliot's Quest for Values*. Detroit: Wayne State University Press, 1965. (The first full-length study, and still probably the fullest and most lucid account of George Eliot's intellectual and religious development, and the thinkers and ideas which influenced her.)

Pascal, Roy (1977) *The Dual Voice: Free indirect speech and its functioning in the nineteenth-century European Novel*. Manchester: Manchester University Press.

Witmeyer, Hugh (1979) *George Eliot and the Visual Arts*. New Haven and London: Yale University Press. (Study of George Eliot's engagement with art, the method and aesthetic of her novels, and allusion to the pictorial arts in *Middlemarch*.)

Wright, T. R. (1991) *George Eliot's Middlemarch*. Hemel Hempstead: Harvester Wheatsheaf.

The following works offer a range of perspectives on literary realism:

Belsey, Catherine (1980) *Critical Practice*. London: Methuen.

Ermarths, Elizabeth Deeds (1983) *Realism and Consensus in the English Novel*. Princeton, NJ: Princeton University Press.

Furst, Lilian R. (ed.) (1992) *Realism*. London: Longman.

Stern, J. P. (1973) *On Realism*. London: Routledge and Kegan Paul.

Tallis, Raymond (1988) *In Defence of Realism*. London: Edward Arnold.

CHAPTER 3: READING *MIDDLEMARCH*

Barrett, Dorothea (1989) *Vocation and Desire: George Eliot's Heroines*. London and New York: Routledge.

Beer, Gillian (1983) *Darwin's Plots: Evolutionary Narrative in Darwin, George Eliot and Nineteenth-Century Fiction*. London: Routledge and Kegan Paul. (Immensely influential contribution to George Eliot scholarship.)

Blake, Kathleen (1983) *Love and the Woman Question in Victorian Literature*. Brighton: Harvester Press.

Carroll, David (1992) *George Eliot and the Conflict of Interpretations*. Cambridge: Cambridge University Press. (Study of George Eliot's work in relation to hermeneutics.)

Chase, Karen (1991) *George Eliot: Middlemarch*. Cambridge: Cambridge University Press.

Creeger, George R. (ed.) (1970), *George Eliot: A Collection of Critical Essays*. Englewood Cliffs, NJ: Prentice-Hall. (Contains ten very useful essays, including: Bernard J. Paris, 'George Eliot's Religion of Humanity'; Barbara Hardy, 'The Moment of Disenchantment in George Eliot's Novels'; U. C. Knoepflmacher, 'George Eliot, Feuerbach and the Question of Criticism'; Quentin Anderson, 'George Eliot in *Middlemarch*'.)

Davis, Philip (1983) *Memory and Writing from Wordsworth to Lawrence.* Liverpool: Liverpool University Press. (Highly engaging reading of George Eliot's work in relation to nineteenth-century secularization.)

Dentith, Simon (1986) *George Eliot. New Readings.* Brighton: Harvester Press. (Useful full-length study of the novels, which considers them in relation to their socio-historical context and nineteenth-century thought.)

Hardy, Barbara (1970) *Critical Essays on George Eliot.* London: Routledge and Kegan Paul. (Includes: W. J. Harvey, 'Idea and Image in the Novels of George Eliot'.)

Holloway, John (1962) *The Victorian Sage.* London: Archon Books.

McSweeney, Kerry (1984) *Middlemarch.* London: Allen and Unwin. (Full critical introduction to the novel, designed for undergraduate students.)

Mintz, Alan (1878) *George Eliot and the Novel of Vocation.* Cambridge, MA: Harvard University Press. (Explores how replacement of the ideal of the religious life by the ideal of vocation in Victorian society informs George Eliot's work, and *Middlemarch* in particular.)

Smith, Anne (1980) *Centenary Essays and an Unpublished Fragment.* Totowa, NJ: Barnes and Noble. (Contains three useful essays bearing on *Middlemarch*, including George Levine, 'The Hero as Dilettante: *Middlemarch* and *Nostromo*'.)

Swindon, Patrick (1972), *Middlemarch. Casebook Series.* London: Macmillan. (Still useful survey of critical opinion of George Eliot including selections from Kettle, Anderson, Harvey, Hardy, and Laurence Lerner's rebuttal of Leavis's criticisms of *Middlemarch*, 'Dorothea and the Theresa-Complex'.)

Thale, Jerome (1962) *The Novels of George Eliot.* New York: Columbia University Press.

Welsh, Alexander (1985) *George Eliot and Blackmail.* Cambridge, MA: Harvard University Press. (Important chapter on 'Knowledge in *Middlemarch*'.)

CHAPTER 4: CRITICAL RECEPTION AND PUBLISHING HISTORY

Carroll, David (ed.) (1971) *George Eliot: The Critical Heritage.* London: Routledge and Kegan Paul, 1971. (Invaluable guide to the contemporary reception of George Eliot's work. Includes reviews of *Middlemarch* from Hutton, Simcox, Colvin, James, Saintsbury and Stephen.)

Foster, Shirley (1985) *Victorian Women's Fiction: Marriage, Freedom and the Individual.* London and Sydney: Croom Helm. (Contains chapter on George Eliot's 'conservative orthodoxy' in relation to the woman question.)

Gilbert, Sandra M. and Gubar, Susan (1879), *The Madwoman in the Attic: The Woman Writer and the Nineteenth-Century Imagination.* New Haven and London: Yale University Press. (Contains highly influential feminist reading of George Eliot's fiction.)

Haight, Gordon S. (ed.) (1965) *A Century of George Eliot Criticism.* Boston: Houghton Mifflin. (Collection of over 50 essays and reviews dating from the publication of George Eliot's first fiction through to 1962, and providing an invaluable survey of George Eliot's critical reputation. Includes reviews of *Middlemarch* from James to Barbara Hardy.)

James, Henry and Gard, Roger (eds) (1987) *The Critical Muse: Selected Literary Criticism.* Harmondsworth, Middlesex: Penguin. (Contains James's important essays on George Eliot, including '*Middlemarch*' and 'The Life of George Eliot'.)

Leavis, F. R. (1973) *The Great Tradition.* London: Chatto and Windus.

Millet, Kate (1972) *Sexual Politics.* London: Abacus.

Moers, Ellen (1976) *Literary Women.* New York: Doubleday.

Myers, William (1984) *The Teachings of George Eliot.* Leicester: Leicester University Press. (Rigorous study that both explicates George Eliot's intellectual beliefs – moral-humanist, social, scientific, and aesthetic – and subjects them to a radical critique via the standpoints of Marx, Freud and Nietzsche.)

Newton, K. M. (ed.) (1991) *George Eliot.* Longman Critical Readers. London and New York: Longman. (Contains useful collection of theorized readings including: Colin MacCabe, 'The End of a Metalanguage: From George Eliot to *Dubliners*'; David Lodge, '*Middlemarch* and the Idea of the Classic Realist Text'.)

Peck, John (ed.) (1992) *Middlemarch.* New Casebook Series. London: Macmillan. (Very useful collection of recent, often theorized, readings, including influential readings by Terry Eagleton, David Lodge, J. Hillis Miller, Sally Shuttleworth and Gillian Beer, as well as Kathleen Blake's interesting discussion of Dorothea's fate in '*Middlemarch*: Vocation, Love and the Woman Question'.)

Showalter, Elaine (1977) *A Literature of Their Own: British Women Novelists from Bronte to Lessing.* Princeton, NJ: Princeton University Press.

Shuttleworth, Sally (1984) *George Eliot and Nineteenth-Century Science: The Make-Believe of a Beginning.* Cambridge: Cambridge University Press. (Crucial contribution to recent George Eliot scholarship.)

CHAPTER 5: ADAPTATION, INTERPRETATION AND INFLUENCE

Booth, Alison (1992) *Greatness Engendered: George Eliot and Virginia Woolf.* Ithaca: Cornell University Press.

Byatt, A. S. (1976) *Iris Murdoch.* London: Longman.

Byatt, A. S. (1991) *Passions of the Mind.* London: Chatto and Windus.

Gervais, David (1994) 'Televising *Middlemarch*', *English*, vol. 43.

Lothe, Jakob 'Narrative Vision in *Middlemarch*' in Chase (2006).

McKillop, Ian and Platt, Alison (2000) ' "Beholding in a Magic Panorama": Television and the Illustration of *Middlemarch*' in Robert Giddings and Erica Sheen (eds), *The Classic Novel from Page to Screen.* New York: St Martin's Press.

Murdoch, Iris (1997) *Existentialists and Mystics: Writings on Philosophy and Literature*. London: Chatto and Windus.

O'Keeffe, Bernard (1994) 'The "Soaping" of *Middlemarch*', *The English Review*.

INDEX